HOW TO CUSTOM PAINT

David H. Jacobs, Jr.

Motorbooks International
Publishers & Wholesalers ®

AE 95-15913

First published in 1990 by Motorbooks International Publishers & Wholesalers, P O Box 2, 729 Prospect Avenue, Osceola, WI 54020 USA

Motorbooks International is a certified trademark, registered with the United States Patent Office

The information in this book is true and complete to the best of our knowledge. All recommendations are made without any guarantee on the part of the author or publisher, who also disclaim any liability incurred in connection with the use of this data or specific details

We recognize that some words, model names and designations, for example, mentioned herein are the property of the trademark holder. We use them for identification purposes only. This is not an official publication

Motorbooks International books are also available at discounts in bulk quantity for industrial or sales-promotional use. For details write to Special Sales Manager at the Publisher's address

Library of Congress Cataloging-in-Publication Data
Jacobs, David H.
    How to custom paint : techniques for the '90s / David H. Jacobs, Jr.
        p.   cm.
    ISBN 0-87938-433-6
        1. Automobiles—Painting.   2. Automobiles—Decoration.   3. Trucks—Painting.   4. Trucks—Decoration.   I. Title.
    TL154.J22 1990.   90-6055
    629.26—dc20   CIP

On the front cover: Mike Sturgeon of Louisville, Kentucky, painted his own 1983 Chevrolet Malibu. He used Corvette Yellow acrylic lacquer in a monochromatic scheme with pinstriping and graphics to accentuate the base of the car; the paint was then covered in clear coat. The Malibu's original 427 ci engine was bored out to 440 ci and is topped by a 1050 cfm four-barrel Holley carburetor hidden beneath the hood scoop. *David Fetherston*

Printed and bound in the United States of America

Contents

	Acknowledgments	4
Introduction	**The Art of Custom Painting**	5
1	**Custom Paint Design and Considerations**	7
2	**Paint Types and Properties**	19
3	**Thinners, Reducers and Support Chemicals**	32
4	**Talking to a Custom Painter or Paint Supplier**	39
5	**Tools, Materials and Safety**	44
6	**Body Preparation**	58
7	**Masking Techniques**	70
8	**Paint Application**	84
9	**Special Custom Paint Tricks and Traditions**	109
10	**Pinstriping**	124
11	**Troubleshooting and Finishing Touches**	141
12	**Paint Care and Detailing**	148
	Index	152

Acknowledgments

This book could not have been written without help from some recognized professional custom painters, autobody paint and supply jobbers and avid auto enthusiasts who shared their special cars. The following people were not only helpful, they displayed an enthusiasm for this project that actually made research and photograph sessions fun.

First off, I want to thank Dan Mycon, owner of Newlook Autobody in Kirkland, Washington. He is truly a car guy and a professional. His expertise in the field of custom auto painting was invaluable. He spent a great deal of time explaining various painting techniques and the chemistry involved with all types of automotive paint and their applications. He was also gracious in allowing a number of photo sessions to be conducted at his shop.

Roy Dunn, owner of Dunn Lettering & Striping in Seattle, Washington, is a talented automotive pinstriper, sign painter and artist. He was patient during photo shoots and always had time to explain the hows and whys for each project. I appreciate his abilities and also want to thank him for locating and securing custom-painted cars for various photo opportunities. It is rare you find a professional custom paint artist willing to share his secrets, so I want to thank him for his time and consideration.

Tim Murdock is the manager of Wesco Autobody Supply in Kirkland, Washington. His knowledge of automotive paint products is second to none. He allowed photo sessions in his store after hours and spent a good deal of time explaining the intricacies of paint mixing, matching and blending. His years of experience in the automotive paint field are noteworthy and appreciated.

Dennis Laursen was an auto painter for twenty years before switching to the auto paint jobber arena as a representative for Bel-Tech Auto Paint of Bellevue, Washington. His insight from both the painter and jobber perspectives was informative, interesting and well versed. Like Mycon, he is a car guy and appreciates quality custom paintwork. I want to thank him

and Brian Keck, manager of Bel-Tech, for letting me spend some time at their store and take pictures.

As an advertising executive for The Eastwood Company, Jim Poluch was able to supply some special painting equipment, along with technical information regarding its operational use and maintenance. I appreciate his helpful spirit and support.

The following folks afforded me the opportunity to photograph their custom-painted cars: Kathryn Mycon, owner of the 1989 Chevrolet Astro van; Dan Mycon, owner of the 1988 Chevrolet sport truck; Roy Dunn, owner of the 1935 Chevrolet panel truck; Bob Thilman, owner of the 1990 Toyota 4X4; Frank Wingert, owner of the 1974 custom Datsun pickup; and Art Sukut, owner of the 1966 Chevy II L–79.

Visiting car shows is always fun, and Steve Brown shared some of his interest in custom cars with photographs he took at a regional custom auto show. He was also helpful during photo shoots and equipment demonstrations. Mike Kane and Mike Link are integral figures at Newlook Autobody, and I appreciate their input and the time they took to help out during photo sessions.

Van Nordquist of Photographic Design deserves a lot of credit for a great job developing the film and processing the prints for this book. He took extra time to make sure every picture turned out just right.

In order to be certain all product information was correct, a good deal of material had to be researched from paint manufacturing companies. I would like to thank the following individuals and companies for supplying much-needed information: George P. Auel from BASF Corporation; Linda Toncray from PPG Industries; Thomas P. Speakman from DuPont; Alan Abbot from Metalflake Corporation; and Jon Kosmoski from the House of Kolor.

Finally, I want to thank Tim Parker, Barbara Harold, Michael Dregni, Greg Field and Mary LaBarre of Motorbooks International. Their continued support and editorial assistance helped to make this an enjoyable project.

Introduction

The Art of Custom Painting

Not that many years ago, automotive paint was manufactured in only one color—black. Automobiles were so new back then, everybody was intrigued simply by the machines themselves; there was no valid reason to further impress customers with special paint or exotic colors. In fact, if the metal used to build those cars had not been vulnerable to oxidation and rust, who knows—automotive paint may have never been invented.

Over the years, though, as more companies started building automobiles and more people began buying them, manufacturers found themselves in a competitive market. Their engineers were directed to design cars with greater style, speed, performance and riding comfort in order to attract a wider range of customers. As time went on and machines became more advanced in dependability and performance, appearance standards began to take on much more significant roles. Now, not only did customers want fast and dependable automobiles, they wanted vehicles that looked different than everybody else's.

The advent of color in the automotive paint industry soon sprang into the picture. In essence, a brand-new field of automobile technology was born. People could buy black cars if they wanted, but could also opt for vehicles sporting a wide range of hues. Before long, two-tone colors were introduced as stock factory options, and the selection of colors grew to enormous proportions. Today, in the 1990s, tens of thousands of different automotive paint colors are easily and quickly available for any vehicle, and paint company engineers are continuing to develop even more.

Not satisfied with stock automobile styles or colors, maverick auto enthusiasts soon discovered that they could alter their personal vehicles to make them look unique and stand alone in a world of similar makes and models. Hopped-up engines, bigger tires, custom bodywork and, of course, special paint colors were employed to drastically change appearance and performance features. Hence, hot rods, street rods and high-performance cars were born.

In a neverending quest to customize cars, auto enthusiasts have gone to great lengths in building special vehicles. As the sheer number of cars on the roadway increased and driving speeds became faster, laws were passed to regulate alterations and keep cars in line with safety and performance standards. Engine, exhaust, drivetrain and suspension systems have to meet strict guidelines in order to be roadworthy. At times, this kind of regulated control can be frustrating for those who want to design and customize exotic machines.

About the only custom auto endeavor free from rules and regulations is paint. As far as I know, you can paint any kind of design or color on your car that suits your fancy. The brightest colors and most psychedelic patterns are perfectly legal, as long as they don't cover windows to obstruct driving ability. They might not be admired by all who see them, but there is nobody around who can tell you they are illegal.

Dan Mycon and Roy Dunn are professional auto painters. Mycon owns an upscale autobody facility and Dunn is a freelance pinstriper and custom artist. Both have been featured in *Hot Rod* and *Sport Truck* magazines. A recent custom paint job was depicted in the May 1990 issue of *Sport Truck*, written by long-time *Hot Rod* editor Bruce Caldwell. The work of Mycon and Dunn is superior and custom imaginations vivid. In the following pages, you will learn some of their trade secrets and how they develop custom ideas and strategies.

Tim Murdock and Dennis Laursen sell auto paint and related supplies. Although actual paint designs are not regulated, use of automotive paint systems has come under scrutiny for environmental pollution and user safety specifications. As color options became more widespread over the years, paint's chemical properties became more scientific in order to make finishes last longer and withstand harsher environments. Both of these gentlemen share their expertise in this field by showing you how to safely and effectively apply a variety of auto paint systems.

The world of custom auto paint is vast and ever changing. It seems that as soon as one painter designs a new wave of graphic and colorful custom options, another inventive painter expands upon the idea to create something altogether different. Where crisp lines

5

and balanced symmetry were the standard a few years ago, dry brush, paint drips, splatter designs and so-called sloppy perfection are the rage in this decade.

This book is not intended to be the last word in custom auto paint. Rather, it is a collection of ideas and paint application methods and techniques that work well for a number of professional custom auto painters and artists. "Basic" is the word here. Not only will you learn how particular designs are affected, you will also discover just what it takes to employ different paint systems and which are better suited for specific occasions.

It is not expected that you will be able to go right out and open a successful custom auto paint business after simply reading this book. However, the information contained here should give you the preliminary means and self-confidence to apply custom paint safely, effectively and with visual appeal. Future endeavors that cross the line from novice to experienced professional will rely upon your practice efforts, imagination, patience and genuine tenacity to learn more about the exciting world of custom auto painting.

1

Custom Paint Design and Considerations

Custom auto painting may be described as anything from simple graphic designs to complete, high-dollar, full-body paint jobs—it just depends upon who you talk to. Dan Mycon, owner of Newlook Autobody in Kirkland, Washington, defines custom paint as anything that varies from a stock design that was originally put on at the factory. Some auto enthusiasts deem subtle graphics, pinstripes and airbrush work as mere add-ons, considering only those paint jobs which employ pearls, candies and exotic colors as truly custom endeavors.

Regardless of definition, all sorts of subtle and elaborate custom paint processes have been used for years by avid auto aficionados in efforts to make their vehicles look special and stand out in a crowd. It's a good thing, too. Just imagine how boring it would be if every hot rod, street rod, sport truck, coupe, roadster and sedan were painted the same. Nothing would be unique because all cars would look alike, just as they do in old black and white movies.

By incorporating various paint applications and stylistic patterns, car owners can make vehicles look entirely different than other identical makes and models. Where auto buffs of years gone by were limited to only one or two paint types and just a few flame or scallop designs, enthusiasts of today are blessed with a huge assortment of colors and a neverending array of new graphic concepts that are limited only by the imaginations of those who dare to venture into the world of custom auto paint.

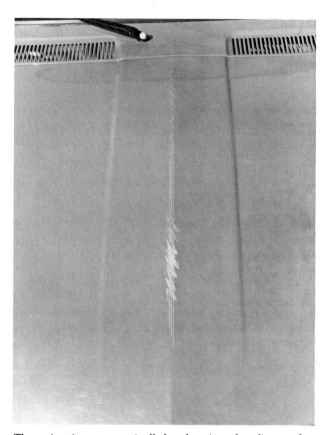

Special paint jobs on customized cars like this 1950s vintage Buick require lots of time for preparation and plenty of skill in application. The light cream color of this car is highlighted around all the trim and the tops of rear quarter panels with light, blended gold. Dan Mycon

Three pinstripes symmetrically break up into short lines as they near the cowling on the pink hood of this Datsun sport truck. A dry-brush pattern is featured in three brighter shades of pink with the middle section closer to white.

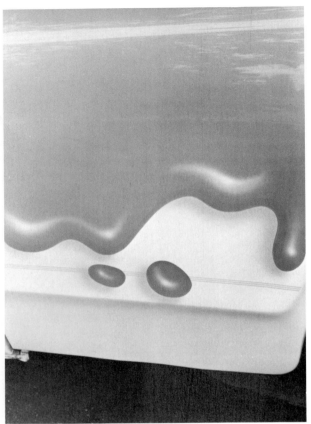

Frank Wingert's 1974 Datsun sport truck is custom painted with three dimensional drops and the splash design. The light section is pink and the dark is green. Airbrush tinting along the edges of drips and drops gives this design its depth feature.

The High Boy on the left sports red scallops over a dark blue body. The one on the right is a lighter blue with pink flames. Years ago, custom paint designs were more or less limited to scallops and flames. Today, custom painters have perfected all sorts of graphic effects utilizing any number of masking techniques, special paint additives and airbrush highlights. Dan Mycon

Vehicle use

Before you jump headfirst into an expensive custom paint project, you must consider your vehicle's actual purpose and how it will be used. For example, if yours is a daily driver that is routinely subjected to parking lot door slammers and gridlock traffic jams, you should shy away from full-body custom paint jobs with candies and exotic multicolor designs. This is because it is extremely difficult to perfectly match these paint applications when repairing small dents or scratches. Even complete panel repaints can result in slightly varied paint additive disbursements or mismatched color shadings.

Custom paint jobs which include candies, metallics or multifaceted designs should be saved for show cars and vehicles that are seldom driven, except for fair weather days, parades and rallies. For all intents and purposes, a show car's exterior paint scheme can be customized to almost any extent because concerns over parking lot mishaps and fender-bender accidents will be almost nonexistent. And since the vehicle will spend a great deal of time under cover, oxidation problems associated with ultraviolet sun rays will be minimal.

On the other hand, automobiles that are relied upon for normal everyday driving are always subject to dings, rock chips, scratches and collisions. For these, you should consider simple applications that are easy to repair with basic paint systems and colors.

Two- and three-tone color schemes can be blended easily to flow with an automobile's body lines to make

This 1990 Chevrolet van was originally painted a solid white at the factory. Custom painting included using thin masking tape on the white, which, when pulled off after the brown was applied, left specific line patterns. Because the color is solid and sharp paint edges separate the design, repaint repairs can easily be made in the case of dents or scratches.

it look unique and stylish. Examples of these are commonly found on sport trucks and vans. Even new car manufacturers recognize the value of two-tone paint schemes as helpful aids to increased model popularity and sales. They have realized that car owners are much more inclined to purchase certain vehicles when they look different than identical models driven by neighbors, friends or acquaintances. The theory? Who wants to own a car that looks just like everyone else's?

Adding a second or third color to a car is not difficult. Body styles generally sport three separate sections that run lengthwise along the vehicle's side. The lowest section extends from the rocker panel to a ridge just about in the middle of the doors. A second section runs from there to the base of windows and the third from glass to the roof. The addition of just one complementary band of color can drastically change a rather mundane-looking vehicle into a more sporty and appealing automobile.

Finding ideas

Perhaps no part of custom auto painting is more perplexing, frustrating and confusing than coming up with specific color schemes and distinctive designs. Years ago, colors were limited and most custom paint work seemed to revolve around flames, scallops and racing stripes.

Today, tens of thousands of various colors are readily available, and custom designs include everything from dry brush to murals, monochromatics to graphics and freak drops to splatter paint. Tim Murdock, manager of the Wesco Autobody Supply Store in Kirkland, Washington, illustrates this dilemma by saying, "Americans just suffer from too much choice."

Special show cars can safely sport a special custom paint job without being subjected to minor fender-bender accidents, rock chips or road debris impacts. You can just imagine how unfortunate it would be to have this deep purple street rod marred with lots of small paint chips or scratches. Dan Mycon

"It used to be that a guy could walk into an auto paint store, order a quart of red paint and leave a few minutes later with just that, a quart of red paint. Nowadays, you have to be much more precise," he says. At Wesco, there are over 600 variations of red auto paint. Unless you ask for a specific color by name or paint code, you'll have to sort through hundreds of color chip pages to come up with a particular shade and type of red.

Murdock boasts that he can supply up to 29,000 different auto paint colors, including antique hues dating back to vintage autos of 1926.

This street rod has been meticulously custom painted in a unique scallop design. The basic color is orange. Front fenders and scallops are pink, with the bottom scallop edges highlighted in a lighter orange. Note the wide white pinstripe used to separate pink and orange colors on the fender and along the top of the scallops. Dan Mycon

Dan Mycon's 1988 Chevrolet sport truck has been painted a monochromatic burgundy. The paint scheme is custom, and because the color is not exotic, repairs and repaint efforts on the dent just below the right taillight can be made easily. Rock chip touch-up and minor scratch repairs are also easily accomplished with this type of custom paint.

A great deal of time was spent applying colorful graphics to this custom Chevrolet Crew Cab pickup truck. Red and yellow graphics surround open areas of black with highlights in blue. The rear fender is red with small lines of a darker red color. Graphics like these are popular and frequently follow specific body lines, ridges and seams to give vehicles a balanced appearance. Dan Mycon

To make matters worse, some paint systems are not compatible with others. Not only do you have to figure out what color you want, you also have to deter-mine which system will safely and securely bond to the paint already in place on your car.

Designs are another matter. Mycon believes that custom painting was initiated by auto enthusiasts who wanted to cover flaws in body and paintwork but could not afford the cost of extensive body repairs and total repaints. Instead, inventive buffs experimented with pinstripes, graphics, cobwebbing, lace, lettering, racing stripes and a wide array of other painting techniques to hide cracked body filler, wavy panels, dimples, wrinkles, orange peel, runs and other paint-related defects. In the process, they not only got rid of an eyesore or two, but they also made giant strides toward the creation of truly custom exteriors for otherwise plain-appearing vehicles.

Ideas from magazines

More than ever, magazine racks are chock-full of auto-related publications. Monthly periodicals carry features that range from definitive descriptions of new cars and their performance capabilities to the latest custom designs developed by noted street rod experts and long-respected customizing innovators.

Mycon's office is filled with issues of *Hot Rod, Truckin', Off-Road, Sport Truck, VW Trends, Petersen's 4-Wheel & Off-Road, Automobile, AutoWeek, Road & Track, Motor Trend* and other auto magazines. He says that the photographs and articles keep him up to date on the latest body and paint trends and also help him visualize certain custom designs when it comes time to

Airbrush highlights in the corners and along the length of this heartbeat design work together with dark highlights just to the left of each upper stroke to bring out a three-dimensional design. Pinstripes were applied using Finesse Pinstripe Stencil Tape, while the heartbeat was outlined with freehand efforts.

Roy Dunn applied his talents to this sport truck using airbrush highlights to separate the green splash design from a gray lower body with black, yellow and white colors. The letter work on the rear window and the Bart Simpson cartoon character on the tailgate were done freehand. Steve Brown

create something really special on a car that belongs to a trend-setting customer.

Roy Dunn, owner/operator of Dunn Lettering & Striping in Seattle, Washington, has an office full of auto magazines just like Mycon. By constantly studying the latest custom paint design trends in magazines, Dunn has been able to stay abreast of rapid changes in the industry. This enables him to apply new concepts almost as soon as they are created. He was one of the first Pacific Northwest pinstripe artists to apply heartbeat, paint drip, splash and dry brush features to cars and sport trucks in the area. At first, folks thought he was crazy. But, as these new southern California trends started to spread across the country, other Northwest pinstripers caught on and now include them in their repertoire of custom auto paint specialties. Because of his tenacity to learn of new ideas and techniques as soon as possible, Dunn got the jump on his competitors and is now known throughout the region as a premiere and innovative professional.

The autobody paint and customizing business is competitive. If the professionals hope to attract new business and maintain lasting customer patronage, it is important they know what trends are popular and which are outdated. Mycon, Dunn and Murdock rely on a number of informational sources to keep them up to date on latest trends and magazines have certainly played a significant role.

To help you discover just the right custom paint scheme for your car, look through assortments of auto publications to see for yourself what is happening in the wide-open field of custom auto paint.

Car shows

In addition to reading about the latest custom paint rage in magazines, attend as many car shows as possible. Interest in automobiles has risen sharply over the last few years and lots of innovative professional car customizers have seized the opportunity to feature their work firsthand at shows in efforts to attract new customers. This allows do-it-yourself customizers to see special vehicles up close and study how particular designs were achieved.

Mycon and Dunn attend as many car shows as they can. They take along a good camera and take pictures of cars detailed with special custom features. Their photos serve two purposes. Entered into business albums, they are used to show customers what types of custom paint jobs could be applied to various cars. Second, pictures help remind painters just how certain designs were laid out and applied. Both Mycon and Dunn study new custom applications to determine just how they were accomplished.

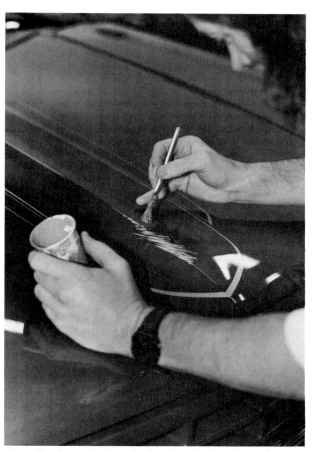

Dunn first learned about dry-brush techniques through magazine articles. Here, he applies a small dry-brush pattern to the hood of a 1990 Chevy sport truck to finish off a pinstripe. He is using a stiff-bristled parts brush and One Shot brand slow-drying enamel paint.

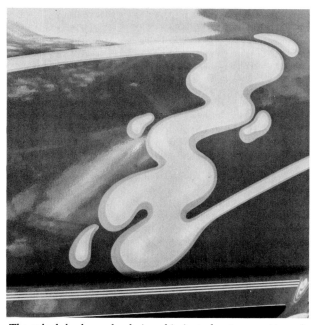

The splash look can be designed in just about any pattern. As part of a heartbeatlike scheme, this splash joins an upper and lower line that runs the length of Bob Thilman's 1990 Toyota 4x4 sport truck. Thin Fine Line tape is used to mask out the basic splash. After this splash has been painted, individual drops are painted by hand and then outlined in a contrasting color.

A small splash decorates a tight spot next to the headlight on Thilman's 1990 Toyota sport truck. Along with a monochromatic paint scheme, splash patterns and pinstripes make this vehicle unique. Note the pinstripes running across the headlight assembly.

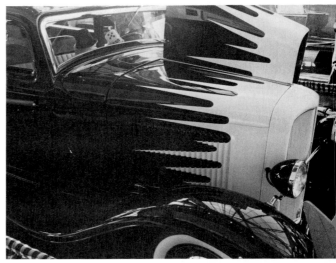

Standard scallops adorn this vintage street rod. Professional custom painters keep track of which paint designs are most popular with certain types of vehicles. Although this kind of scallop design looks great on this car, it might not fare quite as well on a different make or model.

The knock-off feature on this Mitsubishi truck wheel is painted white and has been customized with a pink splatter design. Using a small stiff-bristled parts brush, Dunn simply threw paint at the knock-off to make the splatter effect. Used sparingly and confined to specific masked-off spaces, splatter designs work well to break up solid paint schemes. Steve Brown

Auto magazines are generally loaded with articles and photographs of customized cars and trucks. These periodicals serve as excellent sources for the discovery of new types of custom paint trends. Some of the more popular magazines are Hot Rod, 4-Wheel & Off-Road, Truckin, VW Trends *and* Sport Truck.

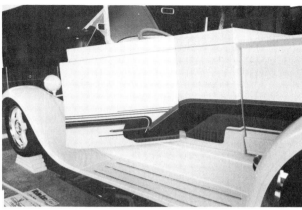

This white custom vintage truck features a unique graphic in dark blue and red. Professional painters are always trying to create new and unique designs, and the professional that applied this graphic is no exception. A great deal of thought must go into projects like this in order to have the final design look clean, crisp and balanced. Dan Mycon

In many cases, custom car owners are seated next to their vehicles during car shows. Take advantage of this opportunity and ask them how they implemented the custom features on their cars. Owners are generally

Dunn uses Fine Line tape as a guide while outlining letters for his business logo on the side of his 1935 Chevy panel truck. Often he actually does pinstripe and lettering work at car shows. This affords onlookers, and hopefully potential customers, the opportunity to see how this work is done and how skilled he is at his craft.

Custom painting is not limited to just cars and trucks. Lots of motorcycle enthusiasts dress their bikes in custom candy, pearl and metallic paint finishes; this is one of Harley customizer Arlen Ness' masterpieces. Bring a camera to auto shows and take pictures of those vehicles featuring paint designs that interest you. It will help you decide what kind of custom effect might look best on your vehicle. Dan Mycon

quite proud of their cars and like to show them off—why else would they be at a car show? Almost as much as they like to admire their cars, they like to talk about them. It would be wise to take along a small notebook and record pertinent information as it becomes available. Combined with your photographs, notes will help

As one design is implemented on a vehicle, other custom painters expand on the idea to create different versions of the basic plan. Professional painters keep these ideas in mind and then return to their shops to try different variations. Using old hoods, trunk lids and door skins as test panels, they are able to test different masking patterns and color blends to come up with unique designs of their own.

Flames are popular custom paint effects on many special cars. This pearl pink High Boy has been tastefully customized with a set of unique flames at the rear wheels. Most of the time, car show displays include placards which list the names of all those who participated in customization efforts; you can contact custom painters named on these cards in order to learn how they effected specific custom designs.

Red scallops over a white body make this sport truck look great. Ideas for custom paint designs can come from many sources. Because of their avid interest in automobiles, members from local car clubs are generally on top of latest custom paint trends and applications. Information about local car clubs should be easy to obtain from auto parts stores, autobody paint and supply stores, auto detailers and painters. Steve Brown

you identify techniques needed to incorporate particular custom designs onto your car.

Car clubs, rallies and races

Auto enthusiasts join car clubs for a number of reasons, the most prevalent being their appreciation for automobiles of particular styles or eras. Along with that, they enjoy various club-sponsored events and the chance to learn more about their special car from knowledgeable and more experienced club members.

During warm summer months, a lot of car clubs and associations hold poker runs, rod runs and rallies. These events often start out with breakfast at a designated restaurant. Afterward, everyone climbs into their special cars and goes for a drive to a lake, beach, park or picnic area. Locations provide ample parking and open space where members congregate, visit and talk about cars. Outings like these provide members with an opportunity to learn more about their cars and about new trends discovered by fellow members.

Notification of club rallies and poker runs are frequently advertised in local newspapers. Flyers are commonly posted at auto parts stores and other outlets which provide auto-related goods and services. Not

The rear door area on this 1990 Chevrolet Suburban has been custom painted with extra-wide pinstripes and a soft blend of color a few shades darker than the body tint. Although the design is not elaborate, it is surely enough to make this vehicle look different than all the rest of the Suburbans on the road.

Painted in a light solid pink, this Volkswagen Bug is accented with a white dash panel and white upholstery. Car club members frequently enter vehicles in local car shows and generally stay close to their entries during a show. This could be an opportunity for you to converse with members about their cars or about membership in their clubs. Steve Brown

A one-of-a-kind graphic has been carefully painted on the hood of this Volkswagen Bug. The painter surrounded blue with a green band and then blended in additional lines of darker blue and orange. Custom-painted cars like this are common entries at car shows. Steve Brown

Broad gold lines accent the trim on this customized Buick. Cars that have undergone extensive body and paint customizing will seldom be driven on the open road. To see them, you will have to attend custom car shows. Regional exhibits are generally held in sports arenas or convention complexes. Dan Mycon

methods for the actual application of custom paint designs.

Auto racing events offer enthusiasts another place where custom-painted cars are available for viewing. For the most part, drag races generally feature more custom designs than circuit racing. Events like tractor pulls, where the likelihood of collisions is not great, may also feature vehicles adorned in beautiful multicolored patterns of exotic paint work, pinstripes, lettering and airbrush scenes. Pit passes for these affairs could well pay for themselves if you are afforded the chance to talk to vehicle owners and mechanics about the custom paint work on their vehicles.

Cost expectations

Too many times, we see cars running around dressed only in a coat of gray primer. One might surmise that its owner cannot afford to buy paint right then, or that the vehicle must be used for basic transportation and the driver is not able to get by without it during the time needed to complete a paint job.

For whatever reason, driving a car covered only in regular primer is not a good idea; many primers are not waterproof and some even absorb moisture, making underlying sheet metal vulnerable to rust and corrosion. About the only exception is two-step epoxy primer. This material essentially seals off surfaces from moisture and other oxidizing substances and will preserve sheet metal until paint operations can be completed.

only can an enthusiast retrieve a lot of good custom paint ideas from occasions like these, they can learn firsthand how other enthusiasts have perfected their

Art Sukut's 1966 Chevrolet II L–79 has not been adorned with flames, scallops, splashes or teardrops, yet it looks custom because the paint job was applied meticulously and has been maintained in pristine condition. If Sukut would have driven the car while it was only primed, moisture could have penetrated the primer to begin rust problems on underlying sheet metal or could have caused blemishes in the paint as it started to evaporate from the primer later.

Just as important as knowing ahead of time what you plan to achieve in your custom paint project is having an idea as to how much the overall effort will cost. Paint and its supportive cleaning and mixing chemicals are expensive, as are rolls of masking tape, paper, tack cloths, respirators and the other tools and materials you will need to properly prepare and paint the car body.

It is not uncommon for professional autobody paint shops to charge $3,500 for a complete paint job. Custom creations can, of course, cost more. The bulk of these fees are directly attributed to the amount of labor involved in just preparing cars for paint. Mycon says that actual painting is the easy part; he even calls it fun. Preparation endeavors, however, account for just about ninety-eight percent of the total labor cost for most paint jobs.

If you already own all of the equipment necessary to prepare and spray a custom paint job, you should expect to spend from $250 to $600 on paint and related supplies for a complete body repaint. The type and quantity of paint, thinner, reducer, primer, sealer, adhesion promoter, sandpaper, tape and masking paper will determine a final cost. If you don't own or have access to paint spray equipment and related tools, you must also consider the additional cost of their purchase or rental.

Costs for applying graphics, scallops, flames and other designs that will simply go over a surface of good existing paint will be much less. This is because you will not need the quantity of paint or related supplies required for a larger job. Still, it is recommended you check with your autobody paint supplier for accurate cost estimates before you start the project to ensure that all required materials will be on hand and ready to use as you need them.

Repair factors

At the beginning of this chapter, repairs were briefly discussed with regard to vehicle usage and specific custom paint types and designs. It would be foolish to spend hundreds and maybe thousands of dollars on a special paint job for a rather ordinary car that will be driven daily through all kinds of weather and driving conditions. This is especially significant when you consider that rather simple patterns using over-the-counter paint will also achieve a custom appearance without the high cost and required hours of labor for super designs.

Custom paint doesn't have to be conservative to be practical. You can design a one-of-a-kind paint scheme that will still allow for spot and panel repair without the intricacies of color blending or matching. Take, for example, a pattern of similar color bands that start as a dark shade at the bottom of the car and gradually rise in succeeding bands of lighter shades. These can be masked at each band with no color feathering and with actual straight-line breaks between each shade. Should a large scratch remove paint from a few bands down to the primer, repairs could be made using identical paint left over from the original job. Masking will keep colors separate and repaint efforts should easily be successful.

On the other hand, let's suppose the same basic pattern was employed but each color was lightly blended into the next, leaving no definitive edge between them but rather a rainbow-type feathering of one into the other. It would be nearly impossible to effect the same scratch repair as above without having to repaint the entire panel. And the chances of having that panel match the rest of the vehicle would be minimal at best.

Dennis Laursen, an auto paint jobber for Bel-Tech Auto Paint of Bellevue, Washington, and twenty-year veteran auto painter, explains that custom paint repairs for newer cars sporting pearl paint jobs are intricate tasks. He says that new car manufacturer's paint representatives are telling autobody paint shops that certain pearl-painted vehicles will not support simple spot or panel repaints. Regardless of the size of the repair to pearl painted panels, it is recommended that the entire side of the vehicle be repainted, from headlight to taillight. This is because pearl additives offer a pearlescent appearance to paint, and spot repairs almost never accomplish an identical blend with suspension of pearl additives on the finish. The color shade will not be exact and repairs will be all too noticeable.

Simple pinstripes and a dry-brush design add custom flair to the door of this 1990 Chevy sport truck painted a monochromatic red. Custom paint endeavors for vehicles that will be driven daily must be able to be repaired easily in the case of minor accidents or paint damage.

The use of your vehicle and the amount of time and money you want to put into its paint job are clearly up to you. Spend some time considering various designs and patterns before you actually start the job. Once you complete a custom paint motif on your car, you will want to keep it looking great. Why frustrate yourself later with major repair operations for minor blemishes when you might be just as happy with a varied design that could be easily and quickly repaired should the need arise?

Creativity: Anything goes

More than any other automotive customizing endeavor, a unique paint job stands out most vividly. Custom paint work can be an expression of one's personality or individual outlook on life. Colors and schemes are synergistic—they work hand in hand to make vehicles look "bad," classy, continental, serene, cool, far out or fantastic. You can create a design that stands tall and dares to be different, or subtly blend tones to generate a sense of tranquility. It all boils down to one's own expression of individuality and how he or she goes about showing it.

Mycon says, "Your car is a canvas and you use it to do your artwork on. Do you want to be conservative, flashy? Do what is economically feasible, do your own thing." In the February 1990 issue of *Petersen's 4-Wheel & Off-Road* magazine, editor Tom Bezzi says much the same in his article, "Anything Goes": "The phrase that characterizes the latest trend in truck graphics is *anything* goes! Forget the old rules. Forget about the traditional line between boys' colors and girls' colors. Forget about tastefully coordinated, carefully masked panels.

Forget no-drip, no-splotch tidiness. Forget satin-smooth airbrush work. Anything goes."

So, go to car shows, read car magazines and even pay a little attention to the fashion trends of designer clothes. Dunn keeps his eye on the fashion circle to keep up with the latest color rages. He figures that what's new and upbeat in clothing's fashion colors will sooner or later trickle into the auto arena. He uses these latest tints to accent cars with subtle pinstripes or wild graphics, whatever the customer wants. These are, perhaps, unusual means to acquire ideas on new hues, but colors are colors no matter what they cover.

When you finally arrive at a design and color blend, find an old hood, door skin, trunk lid or refrigerator to practice on. Try different masking techniques and then actual spray painting. Soon enough, you'll get the feel of it and be ready to apply your distinctive creations to the body of your car.

There are plenty of sources for custom paint ideas all around you. Take advantage of them and of the expertise shared by seasoned custom paint veterans who will talk with you. Be logical with cost and practicality, and then be as imaginative and creative as you want to be.

Dunn used this Paasche airbrush system from The Eastwood Company to paint his name on the side of his 1935 Chevy panel truck. Other work was done by hand using Fine Line tape for guidelines. Interesting scalloplike pinstripes are customized with the addition of pink, white and blue splatter paint. Custom auto paint does not have to follow any specific set of rules; this allows you to design and implement any feature you want.

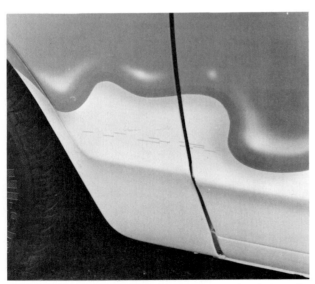

At first glance, it may appear that repainting this design after body damage has been repaired would be almost impossible. However, because solid colors were used inside a definite paint edge (no feathering in of colors) repaint efforts would merely consist of masking and spraying new paint. The airbrush highlights and pinstripes could also be easily applied.

2

Paint Types and Properties

Tim Murdock, from Wesco Autobody Supply, can mix up to 29,000 different automotive paint colors. The BASF Corporation says it has more than 50,000 colors on file and that there are still more colors they can match all the time! In fact, many of BASF's chemists have degrees in fine art and graphic design and use their eye for color, along with computers, to develop new tints and shades as part of an ongoing research and development program.

Paint selection does not stop with simply choosing one or two colors from a roster of 50,000, however. You must also determine which type of paint will be compatible with your car's existing paint, easiest to apply, most durable, cost effective and safest to use. Years ago, painters basically had two choices: enamel or lacquer. Now, auto paint supply stores offer acrylic enamels, acrylic lacquers, urethanes, candies, pearls, fluorescents and more. Murdock contends that auto paint has changed more in the past two years than it has in the last twenty.

Each type of paint carries with it specific properties that make it different from another. Where lacquer is easy to use and quick to repair, urethanes offer long-lasting durability without the need for extensive wet sanding or buffing. Fluorescents are alive with vibrant color, but only stay that way for six months to a year. Candies and pearls are striking in their depth of beauty, but minor spot repairs could require a car's entire side be repainted.

Along with design and durability considerations, you have to understand the various application traits prevalent with different paint types. Some dry in just minutes, others can take days to cure completely and others rely on heat lamps to perfect their finish and resistance to water spotting, environmental pollutants and ultraviolet sun rays. Selecting just the right paint type for your car is just as important as color and design specifications.

Autobody paint and supply store salespeople stay up to date on the application properties and procedures for each paint sold in their store. But they can only guide you through your custom paint purchases if you fully explain the kind of job you are attempting and the

equipment you have at your disposal. Be frank with them from the beginning and get your custom paint job off to the right start.

Paint chemistry

The chemistry involved with the development of auto paint systems is much more complicated than just understanding the application differences between acrylic enamel, acrylic lacquer, acrylic urethanes, polyurethanes and others. You could, if so inclined, get into atomic weight breakdowns and detailed chemical analysis of auto paints through voluminous tomes at the library, but this really won't help you choose or apply specific paint types or colors.

Although learning about the chemical and molecular makeup of automotive paint is unnecessary for the do-it-yourself custom painter, it is important that you understand some of the basic reasons why various paints react the way they do. You then will have a better understanding of why one paint type is better suited for your needs than another. For example, if you applied a

This is just a small sampling of the many color chip catalogs Tim Murdock has at Wesco Autobody Supply. These books feature Glasurit paint products, and the paint chips are categorized according to automobile makes and models. Tens of thousands of different automotive paint colors are available from autobody paint and supply stores.

Used by auto painters to cure paint finishes, these heat lamps come in various styles and feature from one to four lamps per unit. Urethane paints require heat in order to cure to their hardest potential. Most often, newly painted panels are heated to 140 degrees Fahrenheit for about thirty minutes.

Wesco Autobody Supply, in Kirkland, Washington, is a full-service facility that supplies professional body shops and do-it-yourself custom painters with everything needed to complete autobody paint work. Company representatives are highly trained people who keep current with the changing auto paint industry through bulletins and research materials from paint manufacturers.

few coats of acrylic enamel over a lacquer paint job, chances are the job would turn out just fine. On the other hand, should you apply a lacquer paint over an enamel, the paint could be severely damaged and the entire vehicle might have to be completely stripped and repainted.

Solvents, thinners and reducers

The actual materials that make up a paint's color and bonding ability require solvents to keep them in a liquid state so they can be sprayed onto a surface. Since wet paint on a car's surface is useless, the medium used to keep paint pigments liquid must go away somehow in order to let those thin color agents dry and harden.

Paint Components

PAINT	THINNER
VOC SOLVENT (30 - 90%)	VOC SOLVENT (100%)
ADDITIVES	
RESIN	
PIGMENT	

* All that evaporates during spray application and curing, excluding water and a few exempt chemicals, is VOC

What's In A Can Of Paint

A can of paint is made up of four distinct categories of ingredients:

Pigment, which is the color.

Resin, which is the binder that gives it the physical properties to coat a surface.

Additives, each aimed at preventing a specific problem like crawling, cratering, marring, etc.

Solvent, which is the carrier for the coating made up of the first three categories. The VOCs are here.

Pigment, resin, and additives make up the "solids" — so a higher solids product means more of these per can and less solvent per can.

Water-borne systems use water, not solvent, as the carrier — so water-borne systems mean less solvent per can. (A much smaller amount of solvent is needed, only as a coalescing agent.)

The ingredients included in a can of paint. VOCs are volatile organic compounds, elements which reportedly contribute to environmental air pollution. Ongoing research is conducted at all paint manufacturing plants to develop paint systems that will not cause pollution problems and will continue to offer high-quality automotive applications. BASF Corporation

These liquid additives are called solvents, which include enamel reducer and lacquer thinner.

Solvents essentially water down paint pigments and bonding agents to the point where they turn into a sprayable liquid substance, which in turn allows them to flow through a tiny paint gun orifice and then smoothly attach themselves to the surface upon which they are sprayed. Afterward, those solvents (thinners) evaporate so that pigments and bonding agents can dry and harden into pleasant-appearing and durable finishes. These finishes not only make vehicles look good, but more importantly keep underlying sheet metal from rusting.

Various paint pigments and bonding agents work best with certain solvents (thinners and reducers). Therefore, the overall chemical make-up of each paint presents painters with different application, curing and finishing results. It is somewhat like comparing different engine lubricants—some are designed to last 3,000 to 4,000 miles and others up to 50,000 miles. The first kind breaks down after a short while and doesn't cost a lot to replace. The other is expensive, has to be initiated into the engine in a systematic sequence and will not last 50,000 miles if mixed with one of the other kinds. Both types of lubricants do the same job, but each has different application and duration characteristics.

Enamel and acrylic enamel

Straight enamel paint was used for years as a production paint because it covered in one or two coats and dried to a glossy finish that did not need to be rubbed out or buffed. The downside was that application conditions had to be just about perfect because nibs of dust or dirt could not be rubbed out, since such a procedure would break the outer paint skin and mar the surface. Imperfections required spot repainting after the initial coat had cured.

Acrylic enamels became available in just the last few years. According to Dennis Laursen, they rapidly gained popularity because of their long-lasting durability and high-gloss longevity. Acrylic (which basically means plastic) enamels offer the same sort of one-to-two coat coverage capability and glossy finish as straight enamels, but are much more durable. They resist ultraviolet oxidation and environmental hazards better because they dry much harder. This harder quality also makes them more resistant to rock chips, scratches and other impact hazards.

Acrylic enamel can be sprayed over most lacquer or urethane paints with no problem, as long as manufacturer's directions are strictly followed for that specific type of application. In most cases, lacquer cannot be sprayed over enamel. This is because lacquer's chemical make-up attacks enamel bases to wrinkle and craze the surface, virtually destroying the finish.

In some cases, you can spray certain lacquers over enamel bases when compatible sealers or primer-sealers are applied first as a base coat for lacquer. If you are contemplating an easy-to-apply, quick-drying lacquer graphic, flame or special design over an existing

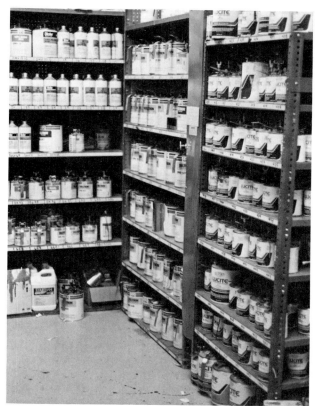

These shelves contain only a few of the various paint products carried by Wesco Autobody Supply. Each product is part of a specific paint system. All paint concentrates and solvents must be compatible or the paint job could be flawed. Color concentrates from these cans are added to quantities of base colors to produce thousands of different hues. This is all done by weight according to computer printout data.

Pink candy flames adorn a dark blue candy finish on this customized street rod. Candy colors are available with different paint types. However, most custom painters opt to apply flame patterns with lacquer because it dries quickly and allows additional color and clear coats to be sprayed on without a long wait. If you want to apply a lacquer design over an existing paint finish, you must determine which paint system is compatible with it. In some cases, specially designed sealers must be sprayed first to protect underlying paint surfaces. Dan Mycon

21

enamel paint surface, you must confer with an auto-body paint supply person first. He or she will be able to direct you to a compatible lacquer paint system that will not ruin your car's enamel paint finish.

Although acrylic enamels sound like great paint products, major concerns have been raised around the chemical hardener that is added to make them dry to hard, durable finishes. These hardeners contain isocyanates, cyanide-based chemicals that are hazardous to painters' respiratory systems and overall health. Every information sheet written about acrylic enamels which require these hardeners advises users to protect themselves by wearing positive pressure, fresh air respirators.

The basic benefits and drawbacks to acrylic enamels are:

Benefits
- One-to-two coat coverage
- No need to rub out or buff
- Dries to a hard, durable finish

Drawbacks
- Long curing time
- Inability to quickly repair minor nibs or flaws
- Contains isocyanates

Lacquer and acrylic lacquers

Before the advent of acrylic lacquer, custom auto painters used nitrocellulose lacquer paint. The basic difference between them lies in their binders, the part of their mixtures that makes pigments and additives bond to surfaces. The old lacquer used a nitrocellulose (cellulose and resin) binder and acrylics rely upon liquid plastic binders.

Older lacquers were brittle and did not fair well against the sun's ultraviolet rays. Plastic binders in newer acrylics are not as brittle and therefore will not crack nearly as easily as the old style. They also include additives which hold up much better against ultraviolet sun rays, thus guarding against early dulling or yellowing of the paint's finish.

Custom auto painters have relied upon lacquer-based paints for use on special designs because of quick drying times, ease of repair and low air pressure application ability. Applying custom graphics or flames requires masking over relatively fresh paint in order to spray bands of other colors on top of or next to the base coat. New masking is also needed, in some cases, for blending in new shades to the design.

With enamel, painters must wait a considerable time before masking tape can be safely applied to a freshly painted surface, even with the use of heat lamps. Since acrylic lacquers dry so fast, masking can begin in as little as ten minutes, depending upon weather, temperature, design and application conditions. This fast-drying feature also helps to make repairs quick and

This classic 1957 Chevrolet has been treated to some unique scallop designs and body alterations. Had it been painted in old nitrocellulose lacquer, the finish would be less resistant to ultra-violet sun rays and more prone to cracking or checking. Acrylic lacquer, which has replaced nitrocellulose, has much better resistance to yellowing, dulling and cracking.

easy. If a particle of dust or debris lands on a wet lacquer coat, you can wait a few minutes for the surface to dry, sand off the nib and then respray.

Acrylic lacquer paint does not require the use of a chemical hardener, which greatly reduces the health and respiratory hazards associated with auto painting. You still need to wear a respirator but can get by with a filter model, as opposed to a fresh air system.

Three to eight coats of lacquer-based paint are required for most jobs. This is because lacquer coats are thin and clear coats will need to be wet sanded in order to bring out the color's deep rich gloss, a quality of good lacquer paint jobs. Since sanding will remove minute layers of paint, plenty of material is needed to work with. Paint manufacturers supply information sheets with their products to help you easily understand just how many coats are recommended when using their particular paint system.

Acrylic lacquer paint systems require a few coats of clear paint over the surface of color coats. When wet sanding, it is the clear coat that is worked on. The color base coat is not touched. This is especially important to understand when applying candy, pearl, metallic and other color-blended designs. If you were to lay down a beautiful graphic utilizing a number of colors all blended into each other, wet sanding would just remove top layers of color and render the graphic plain and dull. When covered in clear, the designed color coat remains untouched, while the clear coat gets wet sanded and buffed to a glossy finish.

The basic benefits and drawbacks to acrylic lacquer are:

Benefits
- Quick drying
- Easy to repair
- No isocyanates

Drawbacks
- Has to be wet sanded and buffed
- Requires more than two coats
- Multiple coats make it vulnerable to cracking

Urethanes

Urethanes are one of the newest types of paint. They combine the durability of acrylic enamels and repairability of acrylic lacquers. For the most part, only a few coats are required for adequate coverage, and wet sanding makes the paint finish even more glossy and brilliant. However, like the acrylic enamels, urethanes require the use of chemical hardeners which contain

Lacquer paint jobs must be covered with coats of clear paint. Afterward, the clear paint is wet sanded and rubbed out to bring out a rich gloss. Not all clear paint products are compatible with all color coats; you must use a compatible product. DuPont manufactures more than one clear paint. Each product has specific applications, and your autobody paint and supply jobber will be able to direct you to the one which is required for your paint system.

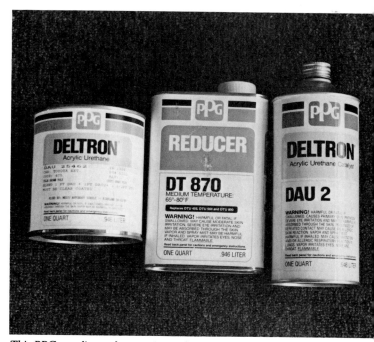

This PPG acrylic urethane paint, reducer and catalyst are part of a paint system. Used together in proper proportions, they will blend to result in a quality paint finish that should last a long time. Application of this type of paint using a catalyst hardener should be done while wearing a positive-pressure respiratory system.

23

isocyanates and mandate that fresh air respiratory systems be used during their application.

Laursen says urethanes "love heat." He means that after painting a car with a urethane product, you should subject the newly painted surface to heat lamps or a paint booth equipped with a heater. Recommended temperatures and baking times are included on all manufacturer information sheets and product application guides.

These paint types were developed for cars of this era. Their durability is exceptional. DuPont's Imron brand is such a paint type. Since it was one of the first of these new breed of paints to reach the auto market, many people mistake the brand name Imron to mean a specific paint type. Other manufacturers produce the same type of paint but label them according to their own specific brand names.

New cars and parts are coated with this type of paint while they are free from associated assemblies and attachments made of vinyl, rubber and other materials that cannot hold up to extreme heat. This is because freshly painted parts are immediately baked at temperatures up to 450 degrees Fahrenheit.

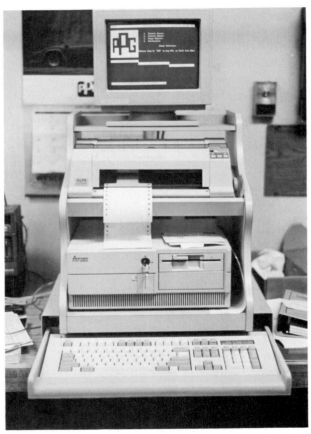

This computer, located at Wesco Autobody Supply, will quickly print out exact mixing proportions for base colors and color concentrates for more than 29,000 different automotive paint colors. Color codes are derived from color chips in catalogs and from paint codes found on automobile identification tags.

The baking process further hardens paint pigments and additives and causes these materials to adhere to the prepared metal surface better than ever before. Mycon and Laursen describe these new paint systems as bulletproof, implying that these finishes can withstand a great deal of abuse and still be polished out to effect a deep glossy shine.

Since this type of paint loves heat, it is important that painters assist curing with heat lamps. Generally, 140 degrees Fahrenheit is recommended; anything hotter may damage vinyl, rubber or plastic parts. Engine computers can also be damaged at higher temperatures. For the most part, urethane paint systems are cured at 140 degrees for about thirty minutes and are then ready for controlled wet sanding.

As with lacquers, urethane paints are applied in a two- or three-step process. The two-step system utilizes a base color coat with a few coats of clear sprayed over the top. Wet sanding affects the clear coat and leaves the color base coat untouched. Three-step systems are required for other, more custom paint jobs. A solid base coat is applied in a certain straight color. After that, a tinted color is applied which, when shot over the base coat, features a unique color shade. After an appropriate number of color coats have been applied and the painter is satisfied with the color and finish, clear coats are put on. Once again, this affords a custom painter the ability to wet sand the clear coat and bring out the desired deep gloss and shine without disturbing base and color coats.

Since urethanes will dry rather quickly with the help of heat lamps, masking off special areas for effecting custom color schemes or graphics is quite feasible. Although professionals have to wait a little longer for urethanes to dry, as compared to lacquer, the durability of urethanes warrants extra patience.

Along with DuPont, most other major auto paint manufacturers, like PPG, BASF, Sikkens, R-M, Glasurit and House of Kolor produce these urethane types of high-tech paint. Although each company professes that their product is best and that their system affords painters the most rewarding results, individual autobody professionals and do-it-yourself customizers have certain brands they prefer over others. Their reasons vary. It could be that particular brands are not available in certain geographical areas or that errors in application techniques caused users to become dissatisfied.

Since auto paint manufacturers must answer to exacting standards, as set forth by various governmental agencies, it is safe to say that most brands really do work well when applied as directed. Of major importance to you, regardless of the paint system used, is that your car's surface be properly prepared and that the application recommendations set forth by the manufacturer are followed to the letter.

The basic benefits and drawbacks to urethanes are:
Benefits
- Durability
- Two-to-three coat coverage
- Can be repaired by wet sanding

Drawbacks

- Contain isocyanates
- Require use of heat for curing

Special paint considerations

Although paint manufacturing companies and autobody professionals may disagree as to which specific paint system is the most outstanding, they all are undeniably united on two critical elements.

First, they strongly advise, and in fact insist, that when using a distinct paint brand you also use that brand's supportive thinners, reducers, primers, sealers and other related products. The reason is simple. Although almost all paints are designed to be sprayed at 70 degrees Fahrenheit and thirty percent humidity, each brand is manufactured with different chemical amounts and properties. The catalyst (hardener) designed for a Sikkens product may not be compatible with a similar PPG material. The same holds true for all paint substances. Their advice is unyielding: Use just one paint manufacturer's system throughout your entire auto paint process. We are not just talking about an actual paint mixture; this advice includes everything from the initial cleaning of your car's body with wax and grease remover through the last efforts of overspray removal.

The second point of absolute agreement concerns overall user safety. Every can of paint and related product carries with it specific safety recommendations.

You are strongly urged to read and abide by these safety instructions. Besides stressing the importance of wearing gloves and goggles, product manufacturers and professional painters are emphatic over their insistence that painters wear the proper type of respiratory protection. Information sheets and product labels will list the types of NIOSH-approved respirators they suggest you use, but you are the one who has to make sure that it is worn.

Asked what advice he wished someone would have passed on to him twenty years ago when he first started in the car painting business, Laursen immediately replied, "Safety!" He was not that concerned years ago about sanding dust and paint fumes. Now he is adamant about the continued and effective use of rubber gloves and respirators and wonders just how his body has been adversely affected by twenty years of body shop dust and paint spray. Retired as a line painter and now working as a paint supply jobber, he feels good knowing that rubber gloves and respirators of all kinds are major selling items at his store. "I'm glad that fellow auto painters are listening to the recommendations of the manufacturers and are wearing their safety equipment," says Laursen. "All it will do is let them live longer."

Candy paints

Enamel, lacquer and urethane paints are specific types of chemical products. Candy paint is not a partic-

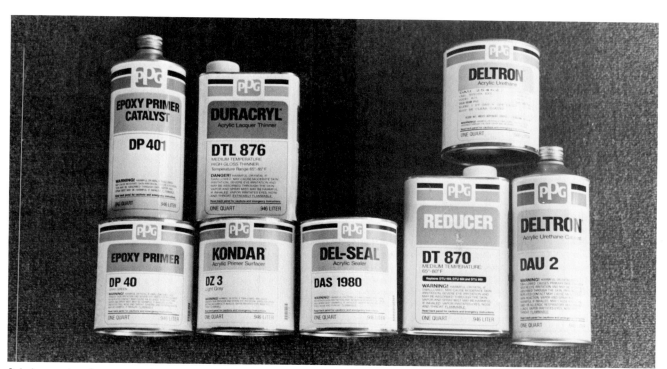

It is imperative that you use just one paint system throughout your custom paint endeavor. This is just one paint system from PPG. It includes, from left to right: epoxy primer and catalyst; primer-surfacer and lacquer thinner; acrylic sealer; and acrylic urethane paint, reducer and catalyst. All of these products are compatible with each other but may not be with similar substances manufactured by other paint companies.

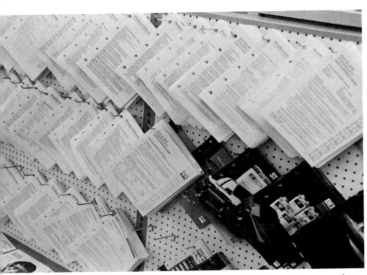

Product information sheets and application guides are abundant at Wesco Autobody Supply. Along with appropriate product usage techniques, these pamphlets supply information about safety and which respirators are recommended when using the material. You should retrieve application guides for all products you plan to use and abide by the instructions featured in them.

Mycon's sport truck suffered a minor dent just below the right taillight assembly. If the truck were painted a custom candy color, it would be almost impossible to spot paint the repair without it being obviously different from the rest of the vehicle. Spot-repair painting for this damage will be easy, as the color is a solid burgundy acrylic urethane.

ular type of paint; rather, it is a different mixture which requires a certain application method, similar to the system used to apply three-step urethane paints.

Custom painters apply a solid base color of gold, silver, black or white to a car. Various colors are achieved by combining certain base coats with specific candy coats. Then, when the base has cured, a mixed blend of clear paint and color toners is applied in succeeding light coats until the desired color is achieved.

The combination of a solid base with numerous light coats of candy paint results in a deep rich color described as translucent. When the desired tone has been reached, coats of clear are sprayed which, when wet sanded to perfection, result in a semitransparent finish of vibrant, deep, rich color. A number of clear coats are required over candy colors in order to protect them from washing, polishing and waxing. The slightest polishing of an actual candy coat will change the color of the section affected. Therefore, clear coats protect color while receiving the brunt of polishing and waxing.

The easiest way to visualize a candy paint job is to hold a lollipop up to the light and look through it. The candy is not perfectly transparent, yet you can see light through it. This is the same effect candy paint colors offer. A base color of gold, let's say, is covered by candy red. Each time a light coat of candy red is applied, the overall color of the car changes. Since clear paint in the candy mix is only slightly tinted, you always seem to see part of the gold base but with more reddish tones perceived with each pass of the spray gun. The more candy tinted passes made, the darker the color, but still always carrying with it a tint of gold.

Candies come in a variety of colors that include red, gold, blue, green, purple and variations mixed in between. Candy toners are purchased as concentrates which are then added to clear. SEM Products recommends their candies be mixed in quantities of four ounces of candy concentrate to a quart of clear, or sixteen ounces to a gallon. Detailed tech sheets are available from the House of Kolor which explain how to mix and apply their custom paint products.

Although candy colors and resultant finishes are really custom, you must understand that repairs are not at all easy. Because a number of candy coats had to be applied in order to reach a desired effect, sanding a spot and repainting it to match the rest of a panel may be impossible. The spot may get just the same number of passes the rest of the car originally got, but feathering in a blend around the spot will cause those surfaces to darken.

Custom candy paint jobs are, therefore, generally saved for show cars and those that are seldom driven in bad weather or heavy traffic. Exceptions may be small panels of custom candy paint added to sections of an automobile, like the hood, trunk lid and certain body panels.

Candy paints are available at autobody paint and supply stores. SEM's Custom Finish paint chip catalog includes twelve candy colors and five bases in acrylic enamel, acrylic lacquer and urethane. Other paint manufacturers, like Metalflake Inc., also offer candy products which allow you to choose the color and system most beneficial for the custom paint job you are contemplating.

Metallic paints

A metallic paint is nothing more than a paint system with tiny flakes of metal added to the clear coat. Small aluminum oxide flakes mixed with a clear coat are visible on top of the color coat and sparkle as light reflects off of them. This style of custom paint was popular in the 1960s and has now become quite fashionable for boats.

A drawback frequently mentioned about metallics is their affinity for reflecting sunlight onto the paint surface on which they are applied. This condition has been blamed for premature oxidation problems experienced by many metallic paint finishes. In addition, as paint oxidizes, metallic flakes tarnish and tend to cause some colors to darken as they age.

Metallic flakes are purchased at autobody paint and supply stores in small bottles. The flakes come in assorted colors and are loose, not contained in a paste of liquid medium. According to directions on the label, a few ounces are added to specific amounts of paint to result in the metallic finish desired. Do not touch metallic flakes with your hand as oils could rub off and tarnish the flakes.

In order to keep flakes suspended in paint mixtures, many custom painters drop two ball bearings into their spray gun cup and shake the paint gun assembly after each pass. Unless flakes are thoroughly suspended in a mixture, their even disbursement on top of a vehicle is compromised. Since these flakes are made of metal, they will tend to sink toward the bottom of a paint gun cup. Maintaining their equal suspension is very important.

Pearl concentrates

Similar in concept to metallics, pearls are extra tiny chips of synthetic inorganic crystalline substances that look like micro-metallic flakes.

Originally, pearl concentrates were nothing more than ground up fish scales added to a paint mixture.

The metallic finish on this car shows flakes dispersed evenly over its surface. To keep flakes suspended in paint gun cups, many custom painters place two ball bearings or marbles in the paint cup and then shake the paint gun assembly after each paint pass. Mixing directions for the paint and metallic flake solution, and air compressor and adjustment settings for the spray paint gun, must be followed to the letter in order to effect a professional-looking metallic finish.

Metallic flakes from SEM, PPG and Metalflake. These are added to clear paint in prescribed proportions to give paint finishes a unique high-sparkle appearance. They are available in different colors from autobody paint and supply stores.

This solution added a different dimension to auto paint jobs in that they actually made parts of cars appear as different color shades when viewed from various angles. Today, pearls are made from tiny chips of mylar plastic which come painted in various colors on one side while clear on the other. Depending upon the color to which it was added, pearls can make just about any paint job look classy and custom.

Pearl material is available at autobody paint and supply stores. It comes in a four-ounce jar mixed in a paste-type mixture. Use a small measuring spoon to retrieve it from the jar and put in a paint mix. Most all the leading paint manufacturers produce pearl additives. They suggest mixing two to four ounces of pearl per gallon of paint. Laursen recommends you start out with two ounces thoroughly suspended in a gallon of paint and then shoot a section on a test panel. As the test indicates, mix in additional small amounts of pearl until the desired finish is acceptable. Just remember, you can always add pearl, but you cannot take it out. Too much will produce a milky finish.

Pearl can be mixed in just about all paint systems. You must check with your autobody paint supplier first to be sure the combination will result in the appearance you want. Used with candy, pearl's reflective nature makes the finish look brighter and more vibrant than ever. Mycon highly recommends you find an old trunk lid or hood to practice on before applying pearl. This allows you a way to test an actual paint-pearl mixture, as well as paint gun pressure and application patterns.

Fluorescents

One Shot brand fluorescent paint is a good product. Its vivid properties, however, suffer from exposure to ultraviolet sun rays, making it become dull after only six months to a year. Although these bright colors have to be clear coated, the sun still renders them dull after a relatively short time. Most custom painters who like fluorescent neons recognize this problem and opt to place them on parts like antennas, roll bars, bumpers and so on in lieu of covering an entire vehicle.

Application can be made with an artist's brush or spray, much the same as any slow-drying enamel product. Be sure to use a clear paint that is compatible when covering fluorescents. And remember that their brilliant nature will not last forever.

Pearl additives are somewhat similar to metallic flakes except that they are much smaller—so small, in fact, that they are contained in a pastelike solution. Pearls come in different colors and are produced by almost all paint manufacturing companies for use in their paint systems. On the left are jars of SEM pearls in red and platinum; the jars on the right are PPG's pearls in bright white and sunset red.

Pearl concentrates come in liquid form. Only a few ounces are added to paint according to mixing directions. Autobody paint jobber Dennis Laursen recommends adding just 2 ounces to 1 gallon of paint and then trying a sample on a test panel. More pearl can be added if needed. On the other hand, too much pearl will cause paint finishes to look milky instead of crisp and clear.

Volatile organic compounds

Air pollution has become a major issue in many parts of the country. Governmental agencies have done much to curtail the amount of airborne pollutants emitted by thousands of companies, and the paint industry is no exception. Volatile organic compounds are chemical substances that rise into the air from paint oversprays to unite with nitrous oxides and produce ozone. Ozone is a major component of smog.

VOCs are basically those elements in a can of paint that evaporate. In the paint industry, solvents are the general term given those chemicals that carry the other ingredients in paint and keep them in a liquid state. After paint has been sprayed onto a surface, solvents immediately begin to evaporate, allowing those other contents to dry, cure and harden. Any gallon of paint may be up to ninety percent solvent. Thinners are 100 percent solvent.

Cities in California, Texas, New Jersey and New York have already passed laws regulating the emission of certain VOCs by local companies. Regulations pertaining to autobody and paint shops require some to install special filtering systems in addition to stock filter components on paint spray booths. Also, many auto paint facilities are now required to use high-volume, low-pressure spray paint systems in lieu of conventional high pressure spray guns. All this is to help reduce the amount of VOCs that are introduced into our atmosphere daily.

Companies like BASF are keeping their research and development laboratories busy trying to develop new paints that can be manufactured without VOCs. Waterborne paints have been produced with mixed results, and research will continue until all avenues have been thoroughly examined. Bob Inglis, director of new product coordination at BASF Refinish says, "By 1992, we'll have to go to a high solids system or the water. As I envision it, it will probably be water-borne for the base coats and high solids for single-stage, solid-shade base coats, and all clears. As far as lacquers are

Fluorescent paints, like SEM's Hotter Than Pink, have gained widespread popularity among auto enthusiasts. The nature of these paint types is such that they start to lose their shine after just six to twelve months. Therefore, most enthusiasts prefer to incorporate these colors into graphic designs and on parts like windshield wipers, antennas and bumpers so that repainting efforts are less intensive.

It is most important to use only those products designed for a specific paint system and to take advantage of all safety precautions when working with automotive paint products. This DuPont clear coat paint will work well with compatible products. Sprayed over an incompatible surface, though, you might find yourself peeling the entire finish off in a single sheet because adhesion was never accomplished.

Get on the R-M stick for a color match •••••••• every time.

These illustrations demonstrate how easy this mixing stick makes your job of color matching by taking out the guesswork.

How to use your R-M mixing stick for MC-1000, 893, RV-86 Clear

It must be mixed with hardener in the proportions shown on the 4:1/2:1 side of the stick.

1. Place stick in straight container with flat bottom, appropriate side facing you for measuring.

2. Pour MC-1000 or 893 2K into container up to (for example) #4 in left hand column.

3. Pour Hardener 894 into container up to #4 in second column.

* Repeat procedure in column 3 and 4 for RV-86 Clear and RV-87 Hardener.

You now have the correct mixture. If more product is needed, pour to a higher number, i.e., #5 using the same method — Clear to #5, hardener to #5, reducer to #5.

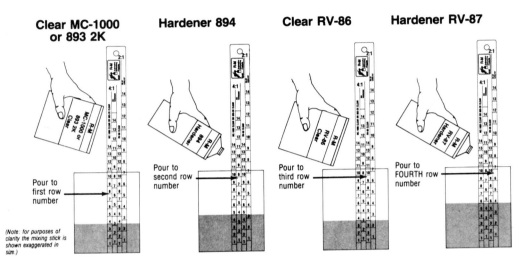

Clear MC-1000 or 893 2K — Pour to first row number

Hardener 894 — Pour to second row number

Clear RV-86 — Pour to third row number

Hardener RV-87 — Pour to FOURTH row number

(Note: for purposes of clarity the mixing stick is shown exaggerated in size.)

How to use your R-M mixing stick for Alpha-Cryl, Miracryl Basecoat

It must be mixed with thinner or reducer in the proportions shown on the 1:1 side of the stick.

1. Place stick in straight container with flat bottom, appropriate side facing you for measuring.

2. Pour Alpha-Cryl into container up to (for example) #4 in left hand column.

3. Pour thinner into container up to #4 in second column.

* Repeat procedure in column 3 and 4 for Miracryl Basecoat and Reducer.

You now have the correct mixtures. If more product is needed — pour to a higher number, i.e., #8 using the same method — paint to #8, reducer or thinner to #8.

(Note: for purposes of clarity the mixing stick is shown exaggerated in size.)

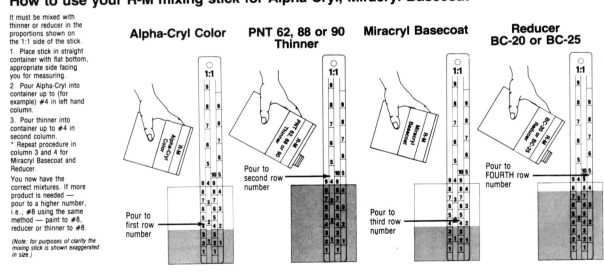

Alpha-Cryl Color — Pour to first row number

PNT 62, 88 or 90 Thinner — Pour to second row number

Miracryl Basecoat — Pour to third row number

Reducer BC-20 or BC-25 — Pour to FOURTH row number

Each manufacturer's paint system utilizes specific mixing sticks for combining the paint, reducer and catalyst. This illustration shows how to mix various brands of R-M brand paint. Sticks depict 1:1, 2:1 and 4:1 ratios. Further instructions on application guides will show you when to use which ratio guide. BASF Corporation

concerned, it's just not conceivable to get their VOC content down to the levels imposed by the new laws. Manufacturers have accepted that lacquers are going to be phased out. Shops have got to accept that also."

The best way to stay on top of the VOC dilemma and to determine which paint system is best for your car is to talk with your local autobody paint and supply store jobber. These people will be the first to know about product changes and will have information sheets from the paint manufacturers describing the ins and outs of the system. Rest assured that any new technology introduced into the auto paint community will be well researched, and compatible systems will be developed for repainting those cars sprayed with what are now conventional automotive paint systems.

High-volume, low-pressure systems

In addition to waterborne paints, technology has advanced in the field of paint spray systems. As Inglis spoke of high solid paint components, companies like Accuspray have developed high-volume, low-pressure (HVLP) paint gun systems that drastically reduce the amount of paint overspray commonly attributed to conventional spray systems. By reducing overspray, VOC emission into the atmosphere is also markedly reduced.

HVLPs only put out five psi but air is warmed to 90 degrees Fahrenheit, and up to ninety-five cubic feet of air per minute is produced. Laursen used an HVLP and was amazed with its performance. He was impressed that it took twenty-five percent less paint to cover the

car and couldn't believe the dramatic reduction in overspray. He estimates there was at least seventy-five percent less overspray using an HVLP unit as compared to a conventional high-pressure spray system. More will be discussed about HVLP systems in chapter 5.

Overview

Determining the correct paint system to use for creating custom paint designs on your car can be confusing. To make things a bit easier, understand that you must determine what kind of paint you will be spraying over. If your car is currently painted with a factory urethane, you can basically spray anything over it. If it is lacquer, there will be no problems covering with lacquer or enamel; check with the autobody paint and supply jobber to see just what urethane can be used. For enamels, shy away from lacquers except for small graphics, and then be sure to apply the right sealer before spraying the lacquer. Check with the auto paint jobber before using urethane over enamel.

If you will be stripping your car to bare metal, you'll be able to spray any kind of paint on the newly prepared surface. Metal will, of course, have to be adequately prepared with epoxy primer and whatever sealer is called for with the system you employ.

Above all else, always talk with your auto paint jobber first, always use suggested safety equipment and always use compatible products manufactured together as a complete system. Never mix brand-name products together; the results could be damaging and hazardous.

3

Thinners, Reducers and Support Chemicals

Information sheets and application guides on all the different thinners, reducers, primers, sealers and other paint support chemicals available to auto painters can be found at autobody paint and supply stores. Every paint manufacturer produces various materials like these for use with each of their specific paint brands. Support chemicals used in conjunction with designated base coats, color coats and top coats combine to make up an entire paint system.

Support chemicals must be used according to the type of paint that will eventually be applied such as acrylic enamel, acrylic lacquer or urethane. The solvents in each chemical must be compatible with the substances in the paint to perfect a final finish. In essence, using the wrong support chemicals would be like trying to mix oil and water.

Besides the basic enamel, lacquer, urethane match-up, you must use those support chemicals strictly designed for the paint system you employ. Mixing a PPG sealer with a DuPont base coat may not work. Whereas, using a PPG system from beginning to end ensures total compatibility for all materials throughout the job.

Most paint companies offer certain warranties with their paint systems. Such a warranty program is offered to professional autobody shops by Glasurit Brand paint, a product of BASF Corporation. A detailed account of Glasurit's warranty is featured in *M-90 Club News,* a pamphlet published by BASF. In it, conditions are listed which explain how a body shop can become eligible for participation in the program. Besides an adequately maintained spray booth, compressor and air dryer, employees of the shop must attend a two-day, Glasurit-sponsored training class and meet other specific requirements. The informational package also states that, "Only Glasurit products specified in the Glasurit Warranty Program book may be used on Glasurit warranty jobs." In other words, warranty shops must use only those components designated as part of an entire specific paint system.

Thinners, reducers and retarders

As described earlier, solvent is a term used to describe that ingredient of a paint mixture which allows pigments and binders to flow as a liquid, enabling them to be sprayed on a vehicle's surface. Once paint has been applied, solvents evaporate to allow pigments and binders to dry and harden.

For all intents and purposes, solvent in lacquer paint is referred to as thinner, and in enamel and ure-

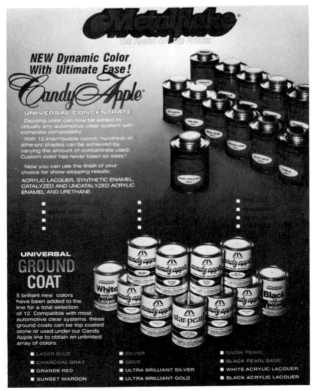

Product application guides, like this one for Universal Candy Concentrate from Metalflake Inc. are important for any custom paint endeavor. This sheet explains that candy colors should be applied first in a horizontal pattern and then in a vertical one, with the third coat applied horizontally like the first. It also explains which primer and primer-surfacer to use and how long you should wait between coats. Metalflake Inc.

thane as a reducer. Both products accomplish the same goal, but are chemically different and affect separate pigments and binders. Each brand of paint product produced by manufacturers has a designated thinner or reducer that is designed to be used with that particular paint. Do not mix brands of thinners or reducers with different brands of paint.

Information and product usage sheets pertaining to the paint system you purchase illustrate how thinners and reducers are to be mixed with particular quantities of paint. Most systems rely upon calibrated mixing sticks which are divided into two or three columns.

On a two-step paint system, the first column designates a quantity of paint—one part, two parts, three parts or whatever. The second column shows how many parts of reducer/thinner or hardener to add. When you fill a container with paint to the numeral 3 on the first column, add reducer/thinner until the entire

mixture reaches the corresponding numeral 3 in the second column. This gives you a predetermined mixture for the paint you are preparing. Each paint manufacturer supplies their own mixing sticks with calibrations matching their paint system.

In a three-step paint mixture system, three columns of numbers are featured. How much paint to put in a container is designated on the first column, how much hardener to add is displayed on the second column and thinner/reducer is measured on the third.

There is another factor to consider pertaining to the properties of thinners and reducers. This relates to evaporation speed. Thinners and reducers generally come in three different temperature (evaporation speed) ranges: fast, medium and slow. For example, PPG's Reactive Reducer used for their Deltron Universal Basecoat Color comes in three ranges suitable for three different temperature ranges: 55–65, 65–75 and 75–90 degrees Fahrenheit. For conditions warmer than 95 degrees it is suggested a retarder be used.

Remember, all paint is chemically designed to be sprayed at 70 degrees Fahrenheit and thirty percent humidity. Variations in those climatic conditions warrant use of different thinners or reducers to achieve paint adherence and curing results similar to those experienced under perfect conditions. For example, on a hot day, you would not want to use a fast thinner or reducer because paint would dry much too fast and probably result in wrinkled, cracked or a nonbonding finish. Conversely, using a slow-drying thinner or reducer on a cold day would result in extra-long paint curing times, possibly resulting in sags and runs.

When discussing your paint project with an autobody paint supply jobber, be sure to point out the conditions you expect to encounter while painting your vehicle. Will you be spraying in a makeshift paint booth constructed in a well-ventilated garage or in a rented

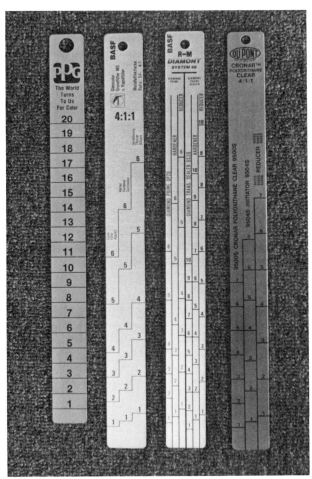

Two-step paint systems only require mixing of solvent with paint; three-step systems require that solvent and catalyst be mixed with paint. To be sure mixing ratios are accurate, paint manufacturers make mixing sticks available. These are samples of mixing sticks from PPG, BASF, R-M and DuPont. Be certain the mixing stick you use is calibrated for the paint system you employ.

R-M brand reducers come in three distinct formulas—slow, medium and fast. These terms refer to the speed in which the solvent evaporates after it has been applied to a surface. All solvents (reducers and thinners) come in slow, medium and fast formulas. Weather and temperature conditions determine which reducer to use. On hot days, slow reducer is used so that paint does not dry too fast. On cold days, you would use a fast-drying reducer.

professional spray booth equipped with a heating system? Temperature and humidity conditions are important to auto paint endeavors, and using the correct thinner or reducer will make a profound difference in the outcome of your project.

Retarders are solvents, just like thinners and reducers. Their function is to slow down paint drying times during extra-hot weather conditions. Various paint manufacturers utilize specific retarders as part of their paint systems. Different temperature ranges are listed under those brand-name retarders, and although they vary in exact degree increments, most encompass conditions from 80 to 110 degrees Fahrenheit. Confirm retarder usage with your autobody paint supply jobber.

Fisheye eliminators

One of the most dreaded problems professional autobody painters face is contamination of painted surfaces by silicone dressings. Silicone-based substances cause freshly applied paint to fisheye, a mar on a finished surface that looks like a popped bubble. In essence, silicone material prevents paint binders from firmly attaching to a surface.

Custom painters face this dilemma when attempting to apply graphics or other artwork near rubber or vinyl trim and bumper moldings that have been subjected to dressing treatments. Many times, silicone remnants are removed by thorough washing with car wash soap and applications of wax and grease removers. In extreme cases, painters must rely on fisheye eliminating additives mixed in with paint.

Mycon and Laursen prefer to spend extra time cleaning and preparing surfaces rather than having to rely upon additives like a fisheye eliminator for problem solving. After extensive cleaning with detergent and chemical wax and grease remover, they use an aerosol glass cleaner. Glass cleaners with ammonia have worked well for them to further remove silicone particles from paint finishes. However, in extreme cases where a car owner has used enormous amounts of vinyl dressing over an extended period of time, they have had good luck using fisheye eliminating products designed for use with the paint system they have chosen.

If you come across an occasion where fisheye eliminator must be used, Laursen and Murdock recommend you use it throughout the entire project, not just on one panel or section. This is so that every part of the vehicle will receive exactly the same paint preparation and will therefore stand the best chance of overall color and finish matching.

Once again, although fisheye eliminators all do basically the same thing, each manufacturer has its own brand name for their product. PPG calls theirs DX 77 Fisheye Preventer, Glasurit has Antisilicone Additive, DuPont's Cronar Fish Eye Eliminator 9259S is for their Cronar brand products, and so on.

Flexible additives

Flexible bumper, front end and accessory components have become common throughout the auto industry. Most of these items are painted at the factory, and many times custom painters like to alter their color schemes when designing a unique new custom finish. For these flexible parts, paint manufacturers offer special flex additives.

According to PPG's Full Line Catalog, their Flexative Elastomeric Additive can be mixed directly with acrylic lacquers, acrylic enamels, urethane modified acrylic enamels and acrylic urethanes to repair flexible body parts. They recommend that parts be cleaned and sanded to promote adhesion of the system. Used with compatible paint products, flexible additives allow custom painters to recoat "soft" assemblies in different colors to produce special designs, patterns and schemes. Additives allow paint to flex with the part to prevent cracking, flaking and peeling.

Each paint manufacturer lists specific instructions for use of their flexible additives with certain paint systems. Be sure to follow directions carefully while mixing paint formulas. Also, be sure to determine what, if any, special preparation must be accomplished before actual painting is started. Refer to information and product usage sheets for guidelines and suggested application techniques.

Primers

Undercoats are those materials sprayed onto a surface to prepare it for the application of paint. Top coats refer to those materials that actually begin to give a surface its final color, namely paint. Undercoats include, but are not limited to, primers, sealers and adhesion promoters.

Without adequate primer coverage, many paint products would not adhere to bare steel, aluminum or fiberglass body parts. Along with the technology that discovered new paint systems and their problem-

PPG's reducers carry temperature ratings on their labels. DRR 1160 is a fast reducer recommended for paint applications when temperatures range from 55 to 65 degrees Fahrenheit. DRR 1170 is for 65 to 75 degrees and DRR 1185 should be used when temperatures are between 75 and 90 degrees.

solving additives, a number of various primer products have been developed.

As with all other paint-related products, each manufacturer produces their own brand of undercoat materials for use with their specific brand-name paint system. And once again, you are advised to stick with just one system throughout your custom paint project.

Epoxy primers, like PPG's DP 40, are designed to be used with a catalyst agent for application onto bare metal surfaces. Products like DP 40 do an outstanding job of protecting metal parts against the effects of oxidation and rust. Auto restorers should absolutely consider using epoxy primers on those metal body parts that have been stripped and that must be stored while work continues on other body parts before actual painting begins.

In addition to being waterproof to protect bare metal against rust, epoxy primers offer excellent adhesion to metal which makes them excellent bases for additional undercoats and top coats. Other catalyst-type primers in the same category as DP 40 are manufactured for similar purposes but are designed for different application surfaces or purposes. Some are made to comply with strict military standards that require excellent corrosion resistance and exceptional adhesion

Epoxy primers, like PPG's DP 40, are waterproof. These primers are excellent products to apply over bare metal surfaces to protect them from moisture, oxidation and rust. The epoxy primer catalyst must be added to the primer in order to make the system work properly. Make sure you follow mixing instructions.

capabilities. Others are made for aluminum surfaces or fiberglass materials.

Although some basic primers are sandable, do not rely on these to fill in surface imperfections like sanding or grinder marks. The two main functions for these kinds of primers are protection against rust and service as an adhesive agent between bare metal and other undercoat and top coat products.

Primer-surfacers

According to PPG's *Full Line* catalog, their DZL Primer-Surfacers are multipurpose undercoats with high solids content. Most other manufacturers have

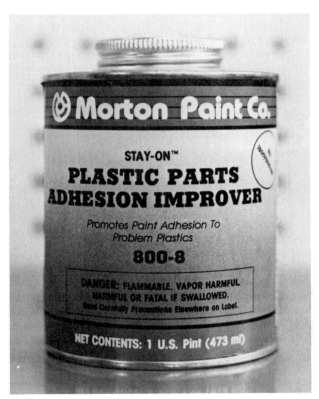

The advent of plastic assemblies attached to auto exteriors created a need for products that would help paint adhere to these nonmetal parts. Morton's Plastic Parts Adhesion Improver is just such a product. In addition to this, flexible additives are available that help paint remain pliable on top of plastic parts, making them less vulnerable to cracking and peeling.

DuPont's gray acrylic primer-surfacer is on the left and red-oxide acrylic primer-surfacer on the right. Certain paint systems and colors may require a particular primer-surfacer color. Loaded with high solid contents, primer-surfacers fill in light sand scratches and other blemishes. When it has dried, the surface is sanded with 300 to 400 grit sandpaper to effect a smooth finish texture ready for paint.

comparable products also designed to fill in minor surface imperfections like sanding marks.

Although some primer-surfacers can be wet sanded with no problems, others are not water resistant and should not be subjected to moisture. In fact, certain primer-surfacers will absorb water. This is important to note for those custom painters who plan to strip old paint and operate their vehicle for a few months in primered condition only. The hazard lies in moisture accumulation. As water becomes trapped inside the porous primer-surfacer, it will eventually find its way to bare metal and start an oxidation process. If an epoxy primer was applied first the metal will be protected, but future coats of paint may be damaged when that trapped moisture works its way back toward the surface.

Custom painters use primer-surfacer after bodywork has been accomplished and epoxy primer applied to guarantee a flaw-free base on which to apply paint. These products contain high amounts of solid substances, like talc, which fill in surface imperfections and allow for finish sanding with fine-grit sandpaper.

Different primer-surfacers are designed for specific applications. While one may be suited for coverage over an epoxy primer and serve as a base for an acrylic enamel top coat, another is to be used on top of fiberglass or aluminum panels for lacquer top coats.

Information sheets carry full descriptions of primer-surfacer characteristics, what kind of surface they are intended to be used on and which top coat paint systems are recommended over them. Autobody paint supply jobbers are also familiar with the intended applications for each variety.

Sealers and adhesion promoters

Auto paint sealers are designed to separate existing paint surfaces from new paint coats. This is an especially important factor when applying new paint that is not chemically compatible with an original paint finish already in place on a vehicle. Sealers also provide a shield between contrasting colors, like painting white over an original black factory paint. PPG's Product Information Sheet (Form P–140) states, "Synthetic primer sealers are specifically designed to provide excellent color holdout and aid in the elimination of sand scratch swelling."

Sealers prevent certain paint solvents from penetrating primer-surfacers and other primers to reduce the risk of sanding scratch swelling and other imperfections. Sealers include certain resins that are not easily soluble in common solvents. There are cases where custom painters will not want particular paint solvents to come in contact with original factory finishes or undercoats. Such would be the case when elaborate lacquer graphics or airbrush work is to be performed on top of an enamel finish.

In addition to helping light-colored shades better cover darker ones and prevent bleed-through, sealers and adhesion promoters assist top coats in bonding much stronger to most surfaces. This is an important trait when considering new custom paint over factory finishes that were baked on at temperatures near 450

PRODUCT APPLICATION
GENERAL PURPOSE PRIMER-SURFACER

1. Reduce 1 part Primer-Surfacer to 1½ parts Metalflake Fast Dry Thinner.
2. Mix thoroughly and strain.
3. Prepare Surface:
   A. If surface is stripped bare, sand with oscillating sander using #180 grit paper. Wash thoroughly with a metal conditioner. Prime with 3 coats of Metalflake Primer-Surfacer. Allow 15 minutes drying time between first two coats and 45 minutes after final coat. Sand with #360 grit sandpaper.
   B. If the existing finish is a factory-baked finish in good condition, scuff with #400 grit sandpaper. Prime with 3 coats of Metalflake Primer-Surfacer. Allow 15 minutes drying time between first two coats and 45 minutes after final coat. Sand with #360 grit sandpaper, and apply a bleeder-sealer before applying a ground coat. Otherwise, we recommend removing the finish to bare metal. (A bleeder-sealer should be used over all primers and other existing finishes.)
4. Prime with 3 coats of Metalflake Primer-Surfacer. Allow 15 minutes drying time between first two coats and 45 minutes after final coat. Sand with #360 grit paper.

This product application sheet for Metalflake's general purpose primer-surfacer is quite thorough. It tells you what the mixing ratio is with the thinner, how long to wait between coats and what grit sandpaper to use after it has dried. Sheets like this are readily available at autobody paint and supply stores for all paint products you will be using throughout your custom paint project.

degrees. Although baked-on finishes are durable and stable, their hard surface quality can be a problem for new top coat adhesion.

Before you purchase a specific sealer or adhesion promoter, check with an auto paint jobber. There are some brands of primer-sealer that can accomplish more than one undercoat function with just one application. For the most part, regular adhesion promoters are invisible and should not affect color qualities.

Wax and grease removers

Before a surface can be covered with an undercoat or top coat, it must be clean. Wax and grease removers are mild solvents used to remove surface contaminants from existing finishes.

Mycon prefers to dampen a clean, oil-free cloth with wax and grease remover, wipe off a section of a car's body and then immediately follow with a clean dry cloth. Using a damp cloth in one hand and a dry one in the other accomplishes a great deal in a short time.

All custom painters clean vehicles first with a wax and grease remover product that is recommended for

the paint system they plan to incorporate. Afterward, some meticulous painters, like Mycon and Laursen, clean surfaces again using an aerosol glass cleaner which includes ammonia. They feel much better about the cleanliness of the finish, and profess that glass cleaner further removes traces of silicone dressing and also helps to evaporate lingering moisture from previous cleaning endeavors.

Paint strippers

Stripping paint is reserved for those enthusiasts who feel existing paint is beyond polishing repair or who have the time and money to change their car's color just because they want to. For the addition of graphics, flames, scallops and a host of other custom features, paint stripping is generally not necessary.

There does come a time, though, when an older car has been repainted too many times. Paint jobs must not be too thick or their appearance becomes less than crisp. Consider stripping paint for complete candy paint jobs and others which will require the addition of numerous base coats, color coats and clear coats.

Custom painters do not have an ironclad rule which determines when paint should be stripped by sanding, sandblasting or chemical paint remover. A lot depends on the car, what type of finish will be applied

Murdock displays a gallon can of PPG AcryliClean Wax and Grease Remover. All surfaces must be clean before the application of any primer or paint product. Wax and grease removers are mild solvents that work fast to remove remnants of silicone dressing, grease, wax and polish. Contaminants on an auto surface will prevent paint from bonding to the surface to result in finish blemishes.

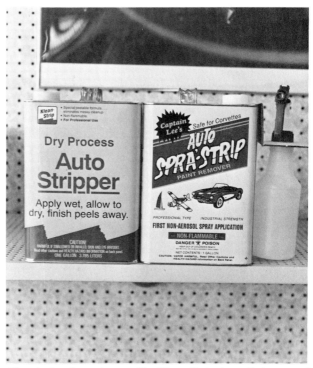

Chemical paint strippers, like Klean-Strip Auto Stripper and Captain Lee's Auto Spra-Strip, work fast to loosen paint for stripping. The process is messy and you should be prepared to properly discard wet paint residue. Safety is a key factor and you must wear heavy-duty rubber gloves during the paint stripping process. Goggles should also be worn to protect your eyes against accidental paint stripper splashes.

During the process of applying a custom paint job, a lot of various chemicals, like lacquer thinner, will be used. Certain hazards are affiliated with each chemical. Warnings are clearly printed on container labels, and application guides include plenty of additional information. If help is needed to decipher the instructions, your autobody paint and supply jobber can assist you.

later and just how thick the existing paint is on a surface.

Most work performed by custom painters centers around processes of surface preparation for undercoats and top coats. Using a chemical paint remover with putty knives may be quick, but putty knives can easily scratch the surface. One also has to consider the introduction of harsh chemicals to weatherstrip material and through openings into concealed body spaces.

Using a chemical paint remover also creates quite a mess, as paint is loosened by the chemical and then peeled away with a putty knife. Residue is soft, wet and somewhat of a chore to clean off of floors and clothes. Consider laying down a sheet of thick plastic before starting the job. When the car has been adequately stripped, fold up the plastic and safely discard.

Safety is a major concern when using any chemical paint remover. You must wear heavy-duty gloves and eye protection. Read label directions carefully and wear an approved respirator as suggested by the label. Cautions about flammability hazards must be strictly enforced. Always make sure the area in which you are stripping paint is well ventilated and isolated from any possible source of ignition, such as pilot lights on natural gas or propane hot water heaters, home furnace units and cigarette smoking.

Overview

Researching every different chemical related to automotive painting can be overwhelming. The easiest way to determine which products you will need is to talk with a knowledgeable autobody paint supplier. If you are not satisfied with the information you receive, stop by a different autobody supply store and talk to that jobber. As with all businesses, some are better than others and some jobbers are more cooperative.

Pay strict attention to all of the safety instructions listed on the labels of various paint chemicals and included on their respective information and application sheets. Certain protective equipment is recommended and its use is highly advised.

4

Talking to a Custom Painter or Paint Supplier

To Dan Mycon, the custom painter, custom means "different." It can be as subtle as painting a Ford color on a GM car or as wild and flashy as anyone can imagine. The decision lies with an owner and his or her use for a vehicle.

To Tim Murdock, the paint supply jobber, custom can mean anything, from an order of 1930 vintage factory paint, to an exotic one-of-a-kind color mixed by hand.

Professionals in both fields must be able to understand customer requests or neither can accomplish the goals set out in front of them. If your request requires an unusual amount of extra time and work to accomplish, expect to compensate those in both fields for their efforts. Above all, be realistic. Both the painter and the jobber are in business to make money. They want your business and will generally bend over backward to satisfy you. But, don't expect a painter to give you a thousand-dollar-job for five bucks, and don't be surprised if a one-of-a-kind quart of super-special hand-mixed paint costs four times that of a stock color blend.

Finding a reputable custom painter

Favorable word-of-mouth comments from satisfied customers have generally been viewed as good indicators of a custom painter's overall abilities. If you do not know anyone who has recently had custom paint work applied to their special car, you will have to do some legwork and find one on your own.

The telephone book's yellow pages are a good place to start. Look under the "Automobile Body Repair & Painting" section for autobody painters that advertise custom work. A phone call should quickly let you know whether or not they can perform the type of service you want.

Since autobody paint supply stores sell lots of paint products to various professional custom painters, you should consider asking them for referrals of conscientious painters. Specialty used car sales lots often know of quality painters and should be able to recommend one. You can even call auto detail shops and performance stores.

Vehicles featured in car shows ordinarily have small signs located nearby that list the names of those who participated in the customizing process. If you like the quality of custom paint applied to one, note the painter's name and then visit the shop for an estimate. Talk to other enthusiasts at car shows. Ask them for opinions about local custom painters, cost estimates and design considerations.

When talking over a custom paint job with a painter, ask to see samples of his or her work. A great many body shop owners keep photo albums close by to show potential customers the kind of work they have done for other customers in the past. Custom paint shops should have a large variety of color photos on hand showing just about every kind of custom job they have ever accomplished. After that, ask to see an actual vehicle they have customized. Look closely for smooth paint edges. Check door handles, window trim, emblems and bodyside molding for signs of overspray. Large blotches of overspray are signs of sloppy work.

Besides the quality of work, you must be able to easily communicate with your custom painter. Designing unique graphics, flame patterns, scallops or other custom schemes will take a cooperative effort. Both of you must be able to understand each other's perception of the final job. If you cannot seem to communicate freely, you might be better off seeking the services of a different custom painter.

Cost estimates

You can generally figure that preparation, masking and painting supplies are going to cost somewhere in the neighborhood of $250 to $600. Regular, long-standing customers of particular paint and supply stores may get discounts but not enough to make any real difference on just one job. On top of materials, professionals must account for electricity, water, equipment maintenance, employee payroll, advertising and a long list of other overhead commitments. This is why shop time is now in the neighborhood of thirty to fifty dollars an hour.

Custom paint jobs include much more than just a few coats of special paint. Preparation assignments can

Reputable custom painters like people to know of jobs they have done. At car shows, their names are usually included on a roster of all who helped to build the vehicle. Cars like this yellow roadster are eyecatchers, and you can bet the painter's name is proudly featured somewhere close by in view of potential paint customers. Dan Mycon

be significant, depending upon what condition the body and existing paint are in. Bodywork might include dent repair, rust management, molding and emblem removal, custom metal work and/or a variety of other things determined by what the final customizing endeavor requires. Old paint may have to be stripped or carefully sanded, either of which takes time. For these reasons, custom paint jobs cost anywhere from $2,500 to $5,000. There are even a few super custom painters whose reputation for outstanding work is in such demand that they charge (and receive) as much as $20,000 for extra-special, one-of-a-kind, super-custom deluxe paint jobs.

Working with a custom painter

Because of the quality and imaginative work they put out on a consistent basis, well-known and popular custom painters are frequently referred to as artists. Novice painters are frequently spellbound by the speed and ease with which experienced professionals apply custom graphics and brilliantly detailed configurations to car bodies. In a sense, some custom painters deserve recognition as accomplished artists because they continually come up with truly distinctive designs utilizing creative and coordinated color combinations.

Custom paint jobs for a rig this size could easily run over $3,000. Rather than spend that kind of money on a super complete paint design, the S&L racing team opted instead for a little artistic work by Dunn. The reverse heartbeat is comple-
mented by a few pinstripes and a wider line at the top. Cost for this was way below that for an elaborate set of colorful graphics or exotic designs.

On a regular basis, though, custom painters normally find that customers already have a good idea of what they want before seeking estimates. With the vehicle in front of them, painter and customer can exchange design considerations and color combinations with quick applications of masking tape and visual comparisons with color charts.

Envisioning a final custom paint job is easy for experienced professionals like Mycon. They keep up to date on the latest trends by constantly reading car magazines and attending custom car shows. They know which colors blend best and are in tune with popular styles of the day. For the untrained eye, though, some help is needed. Mycon responds by quickly laying out basic patterns and designs with masking tape on selected sections of a car and then holding color charts next to them to help illustrate just what a custom job might look like when it is finished.

When you talk with a custom painter, bring along those magazines or pictures that represent the concept or pattern you want applied to your automobile. An experienced painter will explain how such a job can be achieved or if the theme you have selected is better suited for another car style. All vehicles do not necessarily look good with all variations of custom paint effects. Flames, for example, might look great on a 1940s vintage coupe, but awkward on a 1989 Volkswagen Jetta. Graphics in wild fluorescent colors may be all right for some sport trucks, but entirely out of place on a classic 1958 Cadillac Coupe de Ville.

Take advantage of custom painters' experience with design and color combinations. They are just as proud of their work as you are of your car. As much as you want your ride to look special and unique, they want their custom paint job to stand out and be recognized.

Custom paint suppliers

Autobody paint and supply jobbers know a great deal about their products through classes sponsored by paint manufacturers and feedback from the professional autobody and paint shops they supply. Their ability to keep abreast of the most popular paint types and colors is easy because they are the ones who routinely fill custom paint orders from professionals. And, because jobbers frequently visit autobody and paint

This is a rack of BASF, R-M, Glasurit and Diamont paint concentrates. Jobbers use ounces of these concentrates to blend into other base paints in order to develop special colors. Jobbers rely on the business from professional autobody shops to keep them busy with paint orders. Mondays and Fridays are their busiest days, and Murdock suggests you visit autobody supply stores in mid-week for the best chance of finding a jobber with time available to talk with you.

shops during outside sales endeavors, they get to see firsthand what goes on in the real world of custom auto paint.

Few paint jobbers expect customers to walk in off the street and immediately describe the brand, type and color paint they intend to buy. It is their hope that customers realize the difference between enamel, lacquer and urethane, and the wide range of various shades, tints and application procedures inherent with them. When customers understand some of the basic paint properties, it is much easier for the jobber to suggest certain products that are best suited for the job at hand.

Murdock cringes when a customer walks in the door and starts ordering paint products that do not belong together as part of a paint system and then argues with him while he tries to explain the consequences of using a hodgepodge of different brands. He explains that, "Just because his buddy painted a car one time and told him how to do it, doesn't mean either one knows what they are talking about. I will not sell a mix of custom paint and an assortment of inappropriate support chemicals to anyone. They will just end up coming back to me and complaining that the paint I sold them wrinkled, cracked, mottled, bled through or failed somehow, and then expect me to pay for the cost of a total repaint."

On the other hand, when customers explain their lack of experience in painting cars and request help choosing a paint system designed for their expected use and compatible with their car's existing paint, jobbers like Murdock and Laursen go out of their way to explain selected systems and frequently offer helpful advice about preparation and application procedures. They realize custom auto painting preparations can be frustrating at times and recommend that novice painters have plenty of patience.

For this kind of service, both recommend customers come in during slower business hours, like mid-morning on Tuesdays and Wednesdays. They also suggest allotting enough time during the visit to read information sheets and bulletins pertaining to those recommended paint systems supplied by their manufacturers. Note that hectic periods at paint supply stores are generally Monday mornings and early afternoons and all day on Fridays, when professional shops are hurriedly trying to get supply orders in for that week's work, or when they need last-minute supplies to finish jobs in time for the weekend.

Auto paint products may sometimes be purchased at selected auto parts stores or service centers. Except for small vials of touch-up paint, Murdock highly recommends you purchase custom auto paint from stores that specialize in automotive paint products. "Auto paint has become a high-tech business, and novice painters can get into a lot of trouble using products incorrectly or together with incompatible materials," he says. "You don't buy a Chevrolet from a Ford dealer, so why buy custom auto paint from someone who specializes in car parts?"

By the same token, he notes that too many coats of paint are not good. Appearance is compromised and thick films do not flex with car bodies as well as thin ones, usually resulting in cracked paint. This is why multiple coat paint jobs are recommended in lacquer, as their coats go on much thinner than other paint types.

All jobbers may not be able to spend time with customers the way Murdock and Laursen try to do. Some stores are just so heavily involved with local autobody and paint shop concerns that they simply cannot afford it. As you would during selection of a custom painter, attempt to locate a jobber that is easy to talk with and eager to help you during your search for a paint brand, type and color.

Choosing colors

Along with recommending an appropriate reducer or thinner, auto paint jobbers can be quite helpful in color selection. Through experience, they usually know which colors fade fastest, last longest and blend best with existing color schemes. With numerous color chart volumes to look at, they may be able to direct you to just those one or two which catalog the colors of most interest to you, saving time and frustration over multiple choice options.

When a custom color has been selected from a paint manufacturer's chart, jobbers insert that color's identification number into a computer to quickly print out its mixing formula. Using information provided by the formula along with a highly sensitive weight scale, jobbers add ounces of certain color concentrates to predetermined quantities of base color to produce the custom tint chosen.

This method of mixing paint by weight is also used to match factory colors. Formulas are stored in the computer under specific number codes designated for each individual color that was applied at various factories. These number codes can be selected from a paint manufacturer's color chart or determined through vehicle identification numbers found on stickers or metal tags permanently mounted somewhere on every vehicle. For example, Ford numbers are usually on the driver's doorjamb, Toyota and Nissan locate theirs on firewalls, Subaru puts them on radiator support brackets, and so on.

The term matching paint can have more than one meaning to paint jobbers. It is easy to match the factory color on a car by deciphering the paint code on its identification number. On older cars, the original color can quickly be mixed by way of the paint code, but oxidation damage to old paint might require a bit of custom toning to get a new mix to match what is currently on the car. Many times a painter will do this at his or her shop.

Matching the color on a car that has been repainted with an unknown color is done simply by trial and error. In those cases, Murdock will ask customers to pick a color from a stock chart that most nearly matches the paint on the car. Then, he has to add a little of this concentrate and a little of that until he comes up with a perfect match. This is a laborious and time-consuming chore, which results in higher prices for custom, hand-matched mixes.

The same process is used for developing highly unusual, out-of-the-ordinary colors for custom work. If you insist that a paint jobber mix an exotic color not listed on any of the manufacturer's charts in the store or maintained in the computer, you will have to pay more for the special service, as much as $25 per hour. Again, a jobber will have to mix and match by trial and error, since there will be no computer formula to work from. Each time an ounce of concentrate is poured into the mix, it has to be logged so the jobber can keep track of the blend. This takes time, and the longer it takes, the more it will cost.

Murdock highly recommends using only those colors readily available through color charts or computer selection. Mix-and-match exotics cannot be guaranteed to look like what you think they should. He also notes that matching colors from magazine photos and clothing is not as accurate as matching colors already painted on metal surfaces. This is because gloss characteristics are much different on metal surfaces than on other materials. He suggests using automotive color charts as a means to match desired colors from pictures or clothes, thereby allowing you to accurately see what that specific color will look like when applied to an automotive surface.

Overview

Putting a custom paint job on your favorite car should be a worthwhile and rewarding experience. It is not the kind of project you can dream up in the morning and complete by the afternoon. You will spend a considerable amount of time planning designs and choosing colors. Take advantage of any advice you can muster from professional painters, jobbers, customizers, active auto enthusiasts, car club members and the like. The more people you talk to, the more you are apt to learn of new creative and ingenious ideas that you may have never before considered. Combinations from a few of them might turn out to reflect the type of scheme you had hoped to create but had trouble putting on paper.

By conversing with knowledgeable people, you will also become more aware of the thousands of differ-

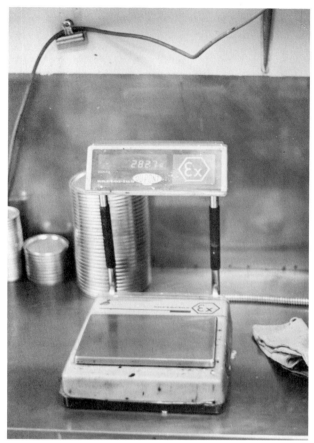

This is a typical scale used to measure amounts of paint, solvent and concentrate for developing special colors. Almost all auto paint is mixed this way. These scales are so highly sensitive that air movement from a simple waving of the hand near them will change its reading. Accuracy is the key to making special colors, and equipment like this makes it all possible.

ent color combinations that are now being used on custom vehicles everywhere. Use this information to help you better communicate with your custom painter or paint jobber. Establishing a good working relationship with either of these professionals right from the start will surely help you in your overall efforts to secure a special custom paint job for your special car.

5

Tools, Materials and Safety

Along with using a dedicated paint system, custom painters realize the importance of using quality tools and materials throughout an entire project. Professionals cannot afford the extra time required to repair equipment- or material-related mistakes and therefore rely upon dependable masking tape, paper, air com-

Cramped for space, this body shop was forced to install its spray paint booth outside under a specially made roof structure. This is a Concept/Cure professional downdraft, heated spray paint booth. It costs around $85,000. Temperature and humidity are controlled, and seals around all doors keep dust and dirt out.

pressors, spray guns and other equipment to get jobs done right the first time. This consideration should also be part of your overall custom paint plan.

Auto enthusiasts tackle their own custom projects for a variety of reasons. Many attempt such ventures just to save money, others simply enjoy hands-on projects and reap personal rewards from their accomplishments. Whatever the reasons, use of inexpensive and ill-adapted tools or materials will cause you grief through extra work and frustrated efforts while trying to make them function as expected. In other words, don't try to get by using the cheapest tools and materials you can find.

If money is a concern, you will be much better off, and a lot happier, waiting a little longer until you can afford to use those items geared for reliable custom painting endeavors. This will allow you to focus your attention on design efforts and paint application techniques, instead of having to continually deal with annoying problems related to masking tape placement, sanding scratches, paint splatter and other frustrating problems.

Work area and homemade paint booths

An ultimate work area might include a brightly lit, dust-free, air-conditioned shop that offers plenty of room and features equipment close by in a neatly arranged series of tool chests and work benches. The paint booth would include a state-of-the-art downdraft ventilation system, a fresh air respiratory system and a temperature-controlled heating system. The only problem is, the cost of such a facility could easily exceed $100,000.

Realistically, do-it-yourself custom painters are forced to use whatever location is available. Most of the time, it is a home workshop or garage. As far as body preparation is concerned, you need an area that is shielded from the sun and will not be too adversely affected by sanding dust or water runoff. Electricity is required for an air compressor and other power tools, and plenty of light is mandatory. A makeshift paint booth must seal out dust and other airborne debris, and also protect surrounding items from paint overspray.

Ventilation is an important consideration, even while wearing approved respiratory devices.

Large sheets of clear plastic can be used to construct a suitable temporary workplace in a garage or workshop. Rolls of clear Visqueen can be purchased at hardware stores and lumberyards. It is important to use clear sheets in order to take advantage of all indirect light. Along with them, you will need strips of lath (thin lengths of wood) and a roll or two of heavy-duty duct tape.

Decide the size of enclosure you need and then wrap the ends of the plastic sheets around strips of lath. Nail those strips to rafters and allow the rest of the sheet to hang down. The bottom edges are secured to the floor with duct tape. If your garage features open rafters, you should consider covering those openings with plastic to keep any dust or debris from falling onto your work surface. Use caution while applying plastic near light fixtures. Even a small amount of heat radiated from lights can damage plastic, possibly catching it on fire.

All paint product labels highly advise users to maintain a well-ventilated workspace. In the case of workshop-type quarters, you should leave garage doors open to allow overspray and other atmospheric vapors to escape. To keep dust and dirt from entering through the open space, thoroughly wet down the area around open doors with a garden hose; you may even need to set up a lawn sprinkler to keep dry areas from becoming dusty. You could also set up a fan in one corner of the front plastic sheet. Seal plastic around the fan's shroud with tape and place a cotton sheet or other suitable filter in front of it so dust is not introduced into the area through the fan blades.

The workplace used for body preparation and masking does not have to be situated in a dust-free environment. Work can take place almost anywhere, although hot direct sunlight is not good.

In lieu of an improvised paint booth, there may be a professional facility available for rent. Auto paint jobbers should be familiar with them and you could also check in the telephone book yellow pages.

Before applying a number of custom base, color and clear coats over an existing paint finish, you may want to know how much paint already exists on the surface. Painting over an existing finish that is in excess of 0.009 in. thick is risky, as extra-thick paint layers can tend to crack or fail prematurely. This Pro Gauge instrument can be helpful. It is calibrated to measure the thickness of paint over existing sheet metal. At a cost of around $35, it is far less expensive than common paint thickness gauges that sell for $200 and up. Pro Motorcar Products

Sanding equipment

Body surfaces must be smooth before the application of paint. Sanding scratches and other imperfections take away from a custom paint job's beauty, making them look non-professional. It is important to use a high-grade sandpaper manufactured for use on car bodies.

Sandpaper

Sandpaper is labeled according to its grit. The lower its number, the more coarse it is. For example, a 150 grit paper is very coarse and will remove a lot of material in a short time. Sanding scratches will be left behind and you will have to use a less-coarse paper for fine sanding. Murdock suggests using a 500 to 600 grit paper to prepare existing body paint surfaces for coverage with custom graphics or other paint designs.

The 1200 grit paper is very smooth; custom painters use it with water to gently rub out small imperfections found on the surface of lacquer and urethane paint finishes. Seldom will the use of 1200 or 1500 grit paper leave deep or definitive sanding scratches; rather, they may present slight swirl-type marks that are quickly removed with polish.

Coarse paper is used to smooth body filler. Medium coarse paper, like 500 or 600 grit, is employed to quickly smooth large blotches of primer-surfacer. Final wet sanding for perfection is done with 800 to 1000 grit paper, switching to 1200 or 1500 grit for finishing.

Sandpaper is categorized by grit. On these sheets, you can see that one is 360, another is 600 and the lighter-colored piece is 1500 grit. This information is standard on the back side of all sandpaper sheets, and additional information will explain if it is a wet-and-dry type, meaning you can use it with water.

The idea is to get the surface as smooth as possible without sanding through primer coats down to bare metal. Sanding is a critical phase in the preparation of car bodies for custom paint, especially when bodywork has been performed. Be sure to take plenty of time getting the surface of your car properly prepared before applying paint.

Sanding blocks

Knowledgeable painters and enthusiasts never hold sandpaper in their hand alone while smoothing a body surface. They always employ some kind of a sanding block. A number of sanding block styles, shapes and sizes are available at autobody paint and supply stores and most auto parts stores.

The palm of your hand and shape of your fingers will conform to the shape of a car body's surface. In addition, the knuckles on the palm side of your fingers present firm bumps, as opposed to the flat surface of a sanding block. When you use sandpaper that is supported by your hand only, irregular impressions are formed on the sanding surface. This will cause sandpaper to dig into a body finish unevenly and result in some parts being sanded too deeply and others not sanded enough. This is especially important when sanding sections of body filler and thick layers of primer-surfacer.

Sanding blocks are flat. As you apply pressure to them, their entire surface maintains a uniform sanding pattern. Only the high spots on a surface are removed. As you continue sanding efforts, feel the surface with your free hand to determine rough spots and where additional sanding is needed. Note how even and smooth the surface feels. If sanding scratches are prevalent, move up to a finer-grit paper.

Sanding blocks of different sizes and shapes are made for sanding efforts on various parts of car bodies.

Wide-based blocks work best on large flat surfaces, like roofs, trunk lids and panels. Smaller and more narrow blocks are best suited for sanding jobs in tight quarters, like between light fixtures and body panel ridges.

In really tight spaces, Mycon uses a thin paint stir stick as a sanding block. Paper is folded over an end of the stick and then gently used to remove imperfections from areas that are slightly rounded or just too small for larger blocks to fit into. As a side of the paper becomes worn out, he tears it off and uses a new fold that was situated underneath. Multiple sandpaper layers folded over a stick not only make it easier to open up a fresh side, but also help to keep the paper in place on the stick.

Power sanders

Power sanders have been used for years by professional auto painters. They do a good job and cut painters' preparation time by significant amounts when compared to hand sanding. Because power sanders remove a lot of material quickly, you must become familiar with them before starting in on the finish of your special car.

Dual Action sanders are fantastic power tools. Instead of featuring a sanding disc that just spins in a

Sanding blocks, like these found at Bel-Tech Auto Paint in Bellevue, Washington, are mandatory for any sanding efforts on auto surfaces. The flat surface on a block prevents uneven sanding that would occur if you used your hand alone. Different sizes and styles are available for various applications.

Scotch-Brite pads are used to scuff slick painted finishes in order to give new paint a decent surface on which to bond. They can also be used to prepare bumpers and trim pieces before painting.

46

circle, DA sanders incorporate an off-center cam that moves the disc back and forth in all directions evenly. Its operation is so smooth, you can hold your hand on the disc while it is operated. On a car body, it quickly sands down rough spots while uniformly smoothing the entire area. If you must perform a lot of sanding work on your car, seriously consider renting or buying a dual action sander.

Masking equipment
Masking tape

Not all masking tape is suitable for car painting endeavors. Although similar-looking tape found at hardware stores and discount outlets appears to be just like the auto masking tape offered at autobody paint and supply stores, the adhesives and paper used in their design are significantly different. Some of the problems you may run across using cheap generic masking tape include adhesive sticking to the car's body after tape has been removed, paint bleed-through on tape edges, higher-than-normal paint edges and lack of strength when stretching tape across long areas.

Murdock points out that masking tape designed for use on cars is chemically treated to adhere to painted surfaces and also to come off of those surfaces cleanly. Autobody paint and supply stores carry an assortment of auto masking tape in various sizes, ranging from ⅛ inch widths to a full 2 inches. The ¾ inch tape is most frequently used in masking to secure paper and cover items such as door handles and trim. For an extensive custom paint job, Murdock suggests having at least two rolls of 2 inch tape and three rolls of ¾ inch tape on hand.

Strips of 2 inch tape are used to cover light fixtures and other medium-sized items, while ¾ inch is used with paper to cover other objects. Expect to pay from

Mycon is using a Dual Action sander to smooth body filler used to cover welds over holes left behind when an emblem was taken off. Dual Action sanders are great worksavers and do an excellent job. Note the ¾ inch tape basically outlining the graphic design that will be applied to Mycon's van. This allowed Mycon to visualize the pattern firsthand before its actual application. Also note the piece of paper taped in place just behind the driver's window. It includes a preliminary sketch of the design Mycon will effect and is used as a guide.

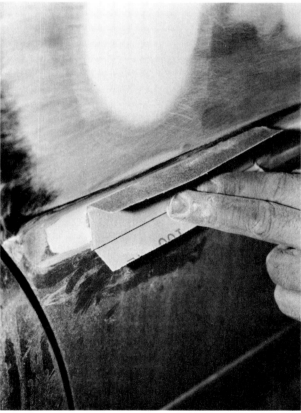

Sanding inside this grooved body section is nearly impossible with a sanding block. In this case, the autobody technician has wrapped sandpaper around a wooden paint stir stick section and then used it as his sanding block. As a side of the paper becomes worn, he simply tears it off and uses a new side.

$1.75 to $2.50 per role for quality auto masking tape. Each roll is 60 yards long, the same length as rolls of masking paper.

Fine Line brand masking tape comes in ⅛ and ¼ inch widths. It is a plastic tape that custom painters use for creating sharp curves and other intricate patterns. Fine Line easily bends around corners much smoother than paper tape. It does not leave creases or folds around corners and adheres flat to allow for clean paint edges. Because it is actually a thin plastic, paint build-up along its edges is minimal, especially when compared to paper tape.

Mycon uses Fine Line masking tape throughout many of his custom paint jobs. After perfecting a design or pattern on a car with Fine Line, he will use ¾ inch tape to attach masking paper to it. The thin pliable nature of Fine Line makes it easy to mask out paint schemes, and its width allows for quick and easy application of tape and paper to it without having to accurately match the exact design. The wider tape must simply attach to the Fine Line somewhere along its width, not necessarily right on the exact masking edge.

Masking paper

Murdock advises never to use ordinary newspaper as masking material for auto painting as it is porous and allows paint to bleed through. Instead, he suggests using paper made specifically for auto masking endeavors.

Found at autobody paint and supply stores, masking paper ranges between 4 inches to 3 feet in width; the 12 inch size is most frequently used. The paper comes in 60 yard rolls, the same as tape. For most paint jobs, two rolls should be sufficient.

If the custom paint job you are planning requires masking off areas measuring from 3 to 8 inches, you should consider the purchase of a roll of 4 inch paper along with rolls of 2 inch tape. It is much easier to mask narrow areas with wide tape or 4 inch paper than to fold or cut 12 inch paper or use strip after strip of ¾ inch tape. Save yourself a lot of extra masking labor by using the most appropriately sized tape and paper for the job. Not only will this save time, it will free you from the frustrations you will encounter while trying to make inadequately sized masking materials do the job.

Rolls of auto masking tape are readily available at autobody paint and supply stores. Different widths are used for various masking projects. The most commonly used size is ¾ inch, while wider rolls work great for quickly covering small and odd-shaped fixtures like lights and reflectors.

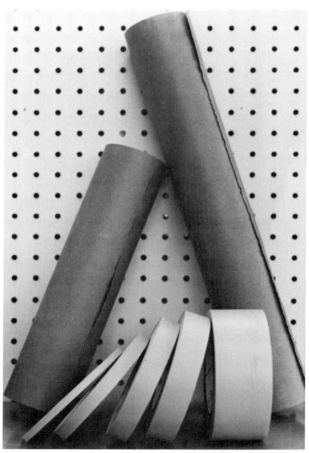

Auto masking paper and tape are designed for use on auto paint projects. Neither paint nor solvent will penetrate either product and the adhesive on tape will not stay on the car after it is pulled. You should have three rolls of ¾ inch tape, two rolls of 2 inch tape and two rolls of paper on hand for your project. Use smaller tape for intricate masking as needed.

Paint equipment
Air compressors and water traps

The information sheets for those paint products you use will specify the cubic feet per minute (cfm) volume and air pressure in pounds per square inch (psi) recommended for its application. Your air compressor should have a label attached to it which signifies its rated cfm and related pressure ratings. This is an important factor in the spraying of auto paint. If the volume and pressure recommended cannot be produced by your compressor, paint will not flow out of the spray gun correctly and will not flow smoothly onto the surface. As a matter of fact, Jon Kosmoski from the House of Kolor believes that nine out of ten paint problems are due to air supply inefficiency.

Most autobody paint shops use compressors with at least a 10 horsepower rating. Professionals like Murdock, Laursen and Mycon recommend that do-it-yourselfers use compressors with a minimum rating of at least 5 horsepower. This is not to say that smaller compressors cannot do small jobs, but they cannot hold up to continued use exceeding their capabilities. When they are constantly used to their maximum potential, problems arise, such as moisture build-up and paint spray irregularities.

Power tools operated by air pressure from your compressor are also subject to cfm and pressure conditions. If your compressor only puts out 6 cfm and the air-driven sander you are using requires 8 cfm, the tool is not working up to its capacity. Moreover, your compressor will be working overtime and the air it produces will be much hotter than normal.

Hot air carries with it a good deal of moisture. As the compressor continues to run, in an effort to keep its holding tank full, heat from continued operation is transferred to internal air. Moisture in the air is then transformed into a steam-like consistency. As air cools inside feeder lines and hoses, actual moisture droplets are formed. Eventually, this moisture will exit through your air tool or spray paint gun to cause problems with tool operation and water splatter on working surfaces.

Be sure to learn what rated capacities are required for the products you intend to spray and what the ability of your compressor is before actually spraying paint. If your compressor is not big enough to handle the load

Fine Line plastic tape works much better than paper tape for making sharp curves and bends on custom paint designs. It does not fold or wrinkle like paper, and it stretches to make application easier. Its extra-thin nature also helps to reduce thick paint edges along masked sections. Autobody paint and supply stores carry this tape in ⅛ and ¼ inch widths.

This is a masking paper and tape stand used at Mycon's New-look Autobody paint shop. It is a handy device that makes pulling off pretaped sections of masking paper a snap. Rolls of tape are attached to small wheels with a section of tape placed on the paper's edge. A spring-loaded bar pushes tape against the paper as it is pulled out and a serrated bar is used to tear the sheet off.

required, consider renting a larger machine from a rental yard.

Every professional autobody paint shop equips its air compressors with water trap devices or air dryers or both. Water mixed with paint products will ruin just about any paint job. Professionals drain air compressor holding tanks and water traps on a daily basis.

An optimum air compressor system incorporates a 5 horsepower, or larger, air compressor outfitted with at least 20 to 25 feet of ¾ in. inside diameter or larger galvanized or copper pipe to serve as extension lines. At the end of the pipe, a water trap is installed. Attached to the water trap is a connection for an air hose which will run to paint guns and other air-driven power tools.

Air lines made of pipe serve two functions. First, they allow for the installation of noisy air compressors outside of the work area with hose connections conveniently located throughout the shop. Second, they allow air to cool inside them and keep droplets of moisture enclosed on their inner walls. Since they are installed with the high point located closest to the compressor

and then run downhill toward a water trap, collected moisture travels toward the trap, not back toward the holding tank.

Laursen and Murdock insist that galvanized or copper pipe is best suited for the installation of air lines. Plastic pipe and air hoses droop and sag in the middle which create holding spots for accumulated moisture. For the home-garage-based do-it-yourself auto painter, they recommend installing an air pipe feeder system utilizing a short piece of air hose to make the connection between the air compressor and pipe. This way, the compressor can be quickly disconnected from the pipe system whenever you want to move it to a different location for other jobs. Kosmoski states that a flexible hose connection between an air compressor and feeder line will also greatly reduce the risk of damage to rigid piping and its supports from the constant vibration of the compressor.

Placing a water trap next to an air compressor is futile. Although some moisture may be confined in the trap, hot air will pass by and moisture will collect somewhere else. If your portable air compressor is stored in one corner of your garage or shop, install a piping system that runs from that location to the other end of a wall. Be sure the pipe runs downhill from the compressor.

Install a quick-connect hose coupling on the end of the pipe closest to the compressor and then a water trap

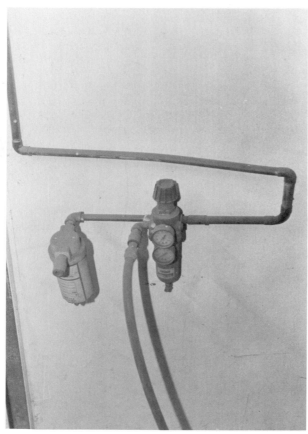

The device on the right is a water trap attached to the wall of Mycon's spray paint booth. In addition to filtering out moisture, it is equipped with a pressure regulator and gauges. Note how the piping is slanted down toward the trap. This is to ensure moisture does not settle in the pipe but rather flows into the trap for future draining. A petcock at the bottom of the trap is used to release trapped water.

A good twenty feet from his air compressor, Mycon also installed an air dryer unit next to the water trap. This device ensures the air delivered to his spray gun is dry and free of any moisture or oil introduced to the system by operation of the air compressor.

and quick-connect coupling to the far end. Use a short piece of air hose, equipped with couplings, to make the connection between the compressor and pipe system. Attach your regular working air hose from the water trap end instead of connecting it directly to the air compressor outlet.

Along with air compressor capacity, air hose size is also a factor. PPG's *Refinish Manual* states, "A three horsepower unit is the smallest size recommended for spray painting of any kind. Use a twenty-five-foot, three-quarter-inch I.D. main line header to reduce moisture if no dessicant drier or air transformer is used. This will help cool the air causing it to lose moisture before the air enters the hose."

This same manual suggests that $5/16$ inch hose is most preferred. The $1/4$ inch hose is too small and creates unnecessary pressure drops between the air compressor and spray gun. It goes on to say that significant pressure drops can be encountered with $5/16$ inch hose when lengths exceed 25 feet. Also, be sure that couplings feature a minimum of $5/16$ inch inside diameter to further ensure no extreme pressure drop experiences.

Paint guns

Conventional spray paint guns come in two basic models, full size and detail touch-up. Full-size models generally include a 1 quart capacity pot and are operated with a gun-like trigger lever. Detail guns are smaller. Their pots usually hold only 8 ounces of paint, and their trigger assembly is mounted on top of the gun, activated by the full length of a painter's index finger.

The difference between these two paint gun models is focused around maneuverability. The smaller gun is more suited for painting in tight spaces, like door-jambs. They offer smaller fan patterns which are excellent for fine work.

The Eastwood Company offers a full range of paint guns, as do most autobody paint and supply stores. You can pay around $60 for a run-of-the-mill paint gun or pay $140 to $200 for a Binks model; cups cost extra, generally around $30. Binks paint gun models have been recognized for years as being one of the best around. A Binks Touchup Gun from Eastwood costs about $130; an aluminum cup is around $30. DeVilbiss and Sharpe are also well-known brands.

Murdock believes in using quality equipment. He says that cheap paint guns do not last long, that their air caps don't always spray correctly and that their fan patterns are bad. He also says parts are hard to find for them. These may be important factors for those who do a lot of spray painting but could be insignificant for the one-time painter. Your plans for the painting equipment you purchase should determine the quality of equipment you buy. The better the product, the longer it will last and the longer it will give you quality service.

High-volume, low-pressure systems

Concern over the earth's environmental decline has caused paint manufacturing companies, paint equipment companies, auto painters and governmental agencies to be more aware of what paint vapors do to our atmosphere. It has been discovered that volatile organic compounds (VOCs) are harmful and that they should therefore be eliminated. In addition to specialized downdraft spray paint booths, professional auto painters in many cities are required to install additional mechanisms designed to reduce the amount of VOCs that escape filtration.

SIZE OF AIR HOSE INSIDE DIAMETER	AIR PRESSURE DROP AT SPRAY GUN				
	10 Foot Length	15 Foot Length	20 Foot Length	25 Foot Length	50 Foot Length
1/4 inch	Lbs.	Lbs.	Lbs.	Lbs.	Lbs.
At 40 lbs. pressure	8	$9 1/2$	11	$12 3/4$	24
At 50 lbs. pressure	10	12	14	16	28
At 60 lbs. pressure	$12 1/2$	$14 1/2$	$16 3/4$	19	31
At 70 lbs. pressure	$14 1/2$	17	$19 1/2$	$22 1/2$	34
At 80 lbs. pressure	$16 1/2$	$19 1/2$	$22 1/2$	$25 1/2$	37
At 90 lbs. pressure	$18 3/4$	22	$25 1/2$	29	$39 1/2$
5/16 inch					
At 40 lbs. pressure	$2 3/4$	$3 1/4$	$3 1/2$	4	$8 1/2$
At 50 lbs. pressure	$3 1/2$	4	$4 1/2$	5	10
At 60 lbs. pressure	$4 1/2$	5	$5 1/2$	6	$11 1/2$
At 70 lbs. pressure	$5 1/4$	6	$6 3/4$	$7 1/4$	13
At 80 lbs. pressure	$6 1/4$	7	8	$8 3/8$	$14 1/2$
At 90 lbs. pressure	$7 1/2$	$8 1/2$	$9 1/2$	$10 1/2$	16

The inside diameter of air hoses can affect the actual amount of air pressure delivered to a spray paint gun. This chart shows some basic pressure drops for $1/4$ and $5/16$ inch inside diameter air hoses when used at specific lengths. Keep these calculations in mind when determining the correct pressure for spraying undercoats and paint so that spray application will be made at recommended gun pressures. PPG Industries

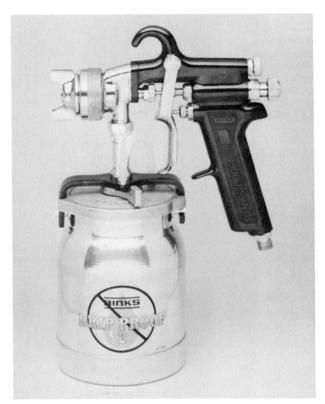

Binks is a widely used and recognized brand of spray paint gun. This brand can be purchased at autobody supply stores and through The Eastwood Company. The two knobs located at the back of the gun just above the handle are used to adjust the fan spray pattern and paint volume. At the nozzle tip, the winged attachment is called an air cap. It adjusts to allow the fan spray to come out in either a horizontal or vertical pattern. The Eastwood Company

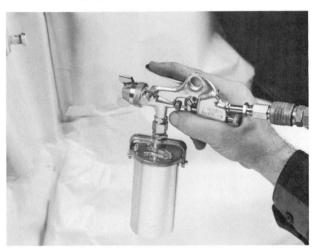

In Eastwood's catalog, this unit is called a touch-up spray paint gun; other painters commonly refer to units like this as detail guns or jamb guns. This is because these small paint guns are very maneuverable and work great for painting small surfaces like doorjambs. Custom painters use touch-up guns for a lot of custom graphics where little paint is required, like for color blending flame designs. The Eastwood Company

Paint manufacturers are working on new, water-borne paint products in an effort to reduce VOCs. At the same time, paint spray equipment manufacturers, like Accuspray, have developed paint application systems that deliver high volumes of material at low pressure. The object of these new paint applicators is to put more paint on the car and less into the atmosphere by way of product overspray.

In the Eastwood Company's *Auto Restoration News,* an article about HVLP systems says, "Conventional high pressure spray painting yields a transfer efficiency of about 20–25%, which means 75–80% of the paint is wasted. To meet new government regulations, heavy industry developed new High Volume Low Pressure (HVLP) paint systems that are about three times more efficient (75–80% efficiency) than traditional sprayers. Quality paint is very expensive, so a 50% savings in materials means an HVLP system will justify its cost with one or two big jobs (such as a house or collector car)." Eastwood's complete models sell for between $650 and $775.

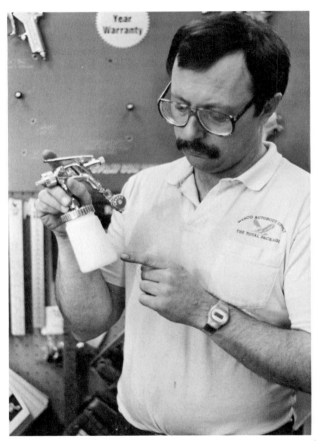

Holding a Sharpe brand detail paint gun, Murdock points out the benefit of having a wide base at the bottom of the paint cup. This allows a user to set the gun on top of a workbench without it falling over as easily as it would if the base was narrower. His right index finger is resting on the trigger mechanism, a flat bar which is operated by resting an entire index finger on it. This is a comfortable and easy type of paint gun to work with.

52

In capsule form, Eastwood's *Auto Restoration News* shows how their Accuspray HVLP system works. "A relatively simple but high speed turbine fan draws air through a replaceable filter. It's forced through several stages resulting in a high volume of low pressure (less than 7 psi) air. Since air heats up as it is compressed, the air that is delivered is warm and dry, ideal for spraying paint."

The report continues, "In 'conventional' high pressure (35 to 80 psi) systems, as the compressed air is triggered out of the gun, it expands. This 'blasting' effect, while good for atomizing paint, also propels the paint particles. The result is overspray, poor transfer efficiency and high materials usage. Too, both the oil and water that conventional air compressors spit out are eliminated. No oil is drawn into the air stream and the turbine delivers constant temperature, humidity, air pressure and volume."

Laursen used an HVLP system to apply a complete paint job to a mid-sized sedan. "Normally," he said, "I would have used a full gallon of paint. This time, it only took three quarts and I was absolutely amazed at the lack of overspray." He went on to say that the job turned out great and he experienced no problems with the system. He believes HVLPs are great for use in home workshops and garages because they reduce paint overspray by at least fifty percent.

As more and more cities develop legislation ruling against auto paint overspray, painters will be forced to employ HVLP systems. A number of custom painters and paint manufacturers have expressed concern over this issue and, for the most part, are pleased that a governmental agency has encouraged an alternative, namely HVLP paint systems. Paint professionals are pleased with the results these paint systems deliver and are also happy that they can paint an automobile using fewer materials. About the only complaint seems to be the concern that low pressure is not well suited for application of pearls or metallics.

If you are contemplating painting more than just one car, you might seriously consider the purchase of an HVLP system. Not only does this equipment deliver dry air, it applies more paint to surfaces and less overspray into neighbor's yards. Besides, the near future may mandate that all auto painting be conducted using such a system.

Safety equipment
Respirators

Until you come down with chronic obstructive pulmonary disease (COPD), you may think the use of filter masks and respirators should be saved for sissies. When Laursen said that he wished someone would have stressed safety on the job to him twenty years ago, he was mainly referring to the use of respiratory protection.

Urethane paint hardeners include isocyanates, which are deadly chemicals. Sanding dust contains elements that your lungs do not want to contend with, and VOCs are bad for the environment so they must be

bad for your respiratory system. Respiratory protection is readily available at autobody paint and supply stores. Laursen says that the store he works for, Bel-Tech Auto Paint, sells a lot of filter masks and quality respirators and respirator filters. "Everyone," he says, "is using respirators now. Everyone."

Paint and paint product labels now carry information about NIOSH-approved respirators. There should be no doubt in your mind as to which type you should be using when painting with certain products. If in doubt, ask the jobber at the autobody paint and supply store.

If you contemplate using paint which requires a hardener that includes isocyanates, seriously investigate the use of a fresh air respiratory system. Eastwood offers Half-Mask and Full-Mask fresh air systems for automotive painters. They range in price from $550 to $750 and include the compressor which operates on 110 volt electricity. For one-time jobs, check with a rental yard.

Gloves

Autobody paint and supply stores require employees to wear heavy-duty rubber gloves when mixing paint; professional painters also wear gloves whenever working around paint products. The reason is because certain chemicals enter your body through your skin. Laursen remembers washing his hands with lacquer thinner to remove paint smudges. He also remembers the skin on his hands being dry, chapped and cracked to the point that they bled easily. Today, if paint should get by gloved hands, he uses 3M Hand Cleaner. It is a product specifically designed to remove paint and still be safe for skin and hands.

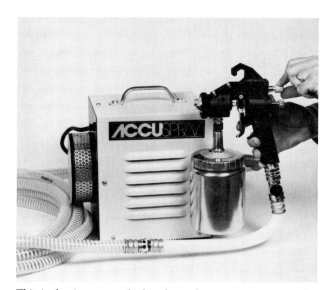

This is the Accuspray high-volume, low-pressure spray paint system available through Eastwood. This handy unit supplies dry, heated air at low pressure and is designed to put more paint on a car's surface and less in the form of overspray. As stricter controls regulate the use of high-pressure spray paint systems to reduce overspray pollutants, use of HVLP systems is envisioned to become widespread. The Eastwood Company

Using products full of thinners, reducers and solvents of all kinds without the use of protective gloves is dangerous. Murdock and Laursen sell rubber gloves to professional painters by the gross. They all realize the potential danger involved with working so closely with potent chemicals and no longer buy the theory of tough-

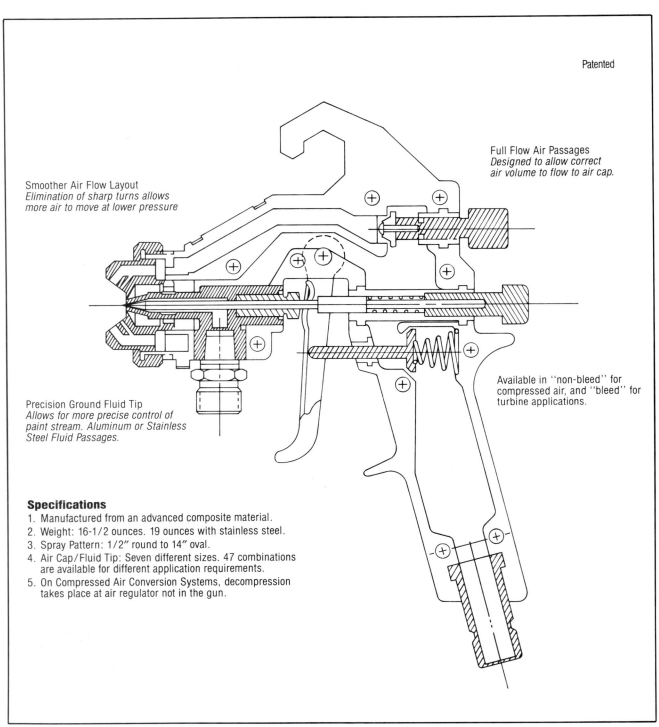

Patented

Full Flow Air Passages
Designed to allow correct air volume to flow to air cap.

Smoother Air Flow Layout
Elimination of sharp turns allows more air to move at lower pressure

Precision Ground Fluid Tip
Allows for more precise control of paint stream. Aluminum or Stainless Steel Fluid Passages.

Available in ''non-bleed'' for compressed air, and ''bleed'' for turbine applications.

Specifications
1. Manufactured from an advanced composite material.
2. Weight: 16-1/2 ounces. 19 ounces with stainless steel.
3. Spray Pattern: 1/2" round to 14" oval.
4. Air Cap/Fluid Tip: Seven different sizes. 47 combinations are available for different application requirements.
5. On Compressed Air Conversion Systems, decompression takes place at air regulator not in the gun.

The anatomy of the Accuspray high-volume, low-pressure spray paint gun. The bleed feature, incorporated into the gun for use with a small turbine compressor unit, allows air to exit the gun at all times. Actual operation and paint application is made the same as with high-pressure guns, except with a significant reduction in overspray and a greater percentage of paint material applied to vehicle surfaces. Accuspray and The Eastwood Company

Environmental Safety Guide

Generally there are different and separate types of body shop environments that you will work in. Each has its own hazards to avoid and more importantly to be protected against. The following is what the well-dressed professional refinisher wears in each of these environments.

- Quality Paint Cap
- Quality Goggles
- Lint-free coveralls
- Nitrile Gloves
- Steel-toed Safety Shoes
- Appropriate Lung Protection

Respirators

Bump Shop
Sanding/Filling, General Surface Preparation Work
Dust Respirator

Spray Booth Environment
Shooting One Stage Primers, Topcoats and NCT quality products
Quality Single or Dual Cartridge Respirator

Spray Booth Environment
Shooting 2-Pack Isocyanate Primers and Topcoats
Quality Air Supplied Mask or Hood

Safety is a primary concern with all paint manufacturers, and it is good to note that most professional auto painters now utilize gloves, goggles and respirators as instinctively as they use spray paint guns. PPG and other manufacturers make various respirators, gloves and paint suits available. They can be purchased at autobody paint and supply stores. PPG Industries

This is an assortment of filter respirators located at the Bel-Tech Auto Paint store and is consistent with displays featured at most other auto paint outlets. Some filters are designed to be exposed to outside air for forty hours and then be disposed of. To keep them in good condition while not in use, they are enclosed in a resealable plastic bag provided with the package.

Positive pressure respiratory systems, like this one from Eastwood, are required for use of urethane paints which use catalyst hardeners that include isocyanates. You must seriously consider buying or renting a unit like this if you plan to spray urethane paint products. The Eastwood Company

ing it out. Quite a number of physical problems can develop due to absorption of chemicals through the skin.

Goggles

Goggles have also become an important piece of safety equipment commonly used by autobody professionals. Even though most airborne debris primarily affect respiratory systems, the absorption of dust and chemicals through porous eye membranes is significant. Grinding and sanding efforts produce large particles of residue which can immediately injure parts of your eye. Other particles, too fine to see with the naked eye, can enter your body through tiny openings and ducts located in and around eye orbits. Long-term effects can be significantly detrimental.

Seriously consider the use of goggles or safety glasses while performing autobody repair and paint work.

Clothes

Although long-sleeve shirts and pants will protect most of your body from contact with paint and supportive paint chemicals, you must be concerned with the effect lint and other clothing debris will have on the surface of your paint job. It would be quite frustrating to apply a beautiful candy paint job on a classic Ford roof, only to have it marred by a piece of lint that fell off a long-sleeved flannel shirt.

Rubber gloves are worn by painters when mixing and spraying paint products. Chemicals in paint and solvents will attack skin to make it dry and eventually crack. The more the skin on your hands is exposed to potent chemicals, the higher your chances become of developing related medical problems. Gloves like these are inexpensive and readily available at autobody paint and supply stores.

Other considerations are belt buckles and rivets on certain kinds of denim trousers. As you lean against your car while painting the roof, hood or trunk lid, are hard projections scratching the side of it? You must be aware of the type of clothing you are wearing while working in such close proximity to the finish of your car.

PPG, DuPont and other paint manufacturers market coveralls made specifically for painters. These suits offer wearers protection against contact with chemicals and also feature lint-free materials that will not shed lint upon paint surfaces. Their cost is minimal and they are readily available at your local autobody paint and supply store.

Safety while painting automobiles is an important consideration. You will be working with highly flammable materials and chemicals which can definitely harm your body. Governmental regulations have required paint manufacturers to provide detailed labels on all their products and have also required them to provide material safety data sheets to all jobbers who carry their products.

The bottom line is, if you are concerned about safety, your autobody paint and supply jobber can give you all the listed safety requirements that manufacturers recommend for optimum user safety.

Face shields and goggles are excellent safety devices that should be worn any time there is a possibility of airborne debris striking your face. Autobody technicians have realized the significance of wearing safety equipment, commonly used during grinder operations, and now commonly wear eye protection during most autobody and paint operations.

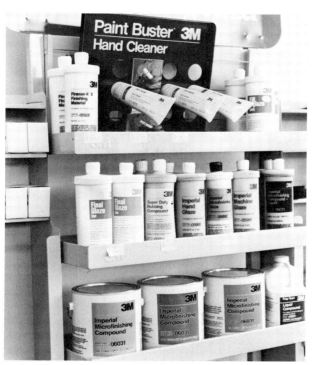

In lieu of washing paint drops from your hands or arms with solvent, opt instead for hand cleaners developed specifically for the removal of paint from skin. 3M's Hand Cleaner works great and is safe for skin. In addition to the hand cleaner on the top shelf, a number of 3M polishing and rubbing compounds are featured. Each type has specific uses, and you must read the label to choose the polish most suited for your needs.

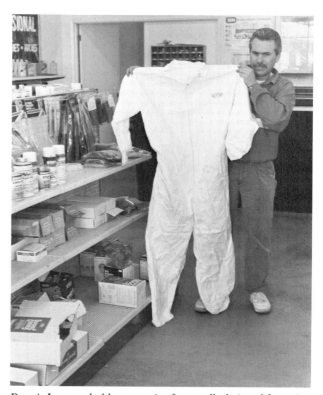

Dennis Laursen holds up a pair of coveralls designed for painters. This outfit is made by DuPont and is available at most autobody paint and supply stores. Made of a special material, these garments resist paint absorption and are also lint-free. In addition to keeping painters protected from overspray, they reduce the risk of lint from clothes falling onto a work surface.

6

Body Preparation

Preparing an automobile's surface for custom paint entails a few basic procedures. These operations pertain to cars with perfect existing paint, as well as those which underwent recent body repair. The finish must be smooth and clean with obstructions properly masked off.

Paint on newer cars does not always have to be removed in order to apply a new custom design.

Mycon is using a soft cotton wash mitt to clean this van. All vehicle surfaces must be clean before any body or paintwork can be started. Air pressure from paint guns could dislodge dirt and grit from behind moldings, drip rails, grille sections and other areas which might land on painted parts to cause blemishes. Cotton wash mitts are gentle on paint and will not cause minute spider-webbing scratches.

Newlook Autobody technician Mike Link uses an air-driven ratchet to remove brackets from a front bumper that is being prepared for paint. Even if the bumper was not scheduled for paint, it would have been removed in order to gain best access to body parts located around it. Removing bumpers is generally much easier than masking and maneuvering paint guns around them.

58

Because paint finishes on late-model cars have been baked on at temperatures of around 450 degrees Fahrenheit, their surface is hard and durable, making them a good base for new paint. Some sanding is required in order to give new paint a good bonding surface.

Older cars that suffer oxidized or otherwise bad paint finishes may have to be stripped before the application of new paint. Stripping will require a few coats of various primers and adhesion promoters before new paint can be sprayed.

Determining the type of paint on your car

In the case of new cars, it is easy to determine what type of paint was applied at the factory by deciphering the color code on the vehicle's identification label. For older cars that have just been repainted, simply consult the painter who did the work. But, how can you tell what kind of paint is on a repainted car when you have no idea when or who repainted it?

You can test paint on such a car with the use of lacquer thinner and a clean white rag; Mycon, Murdock

and Laursen have done this many times. Soak a white cloth with lacquer thinner and rub an inconspicuous area with the wet cloth. If the paint dissolves quickly, it's lacquer; if it dissolves after considerable rubbing, it's acrylic lacquer. If the area tends to pucker or wrinkle, it's uncured enamel. Lacquer thinner will not dissolve properly cured acrylic enamel or urethane enamel.

Going a step further, to ascertain the difference between a base coat/clear coat and a standard color finish with no clear over the top, use fine sandpaper. Rub 800 to 1000 grit sandpaper on a small spot that is out of the way. If white sanding dust is created, the finish is a base coat/clear coat. White dust designates

You can see the amount of dirt that was located behind this emblem and along the backside of bodyside molding. Since the custom paint scheme planned for this vehicle required removal of these pieces, dirt was easily spotted and washed away. For custom paint designs that do not require removal of trim, be sure to run plenty of clear water behind each piece in order to dislodge and float away dust, dirt and grit.

Since Dunn painted this splash design by hand, there was no need to remove the Mitsubishi emblem. Had spray paint been employed, painting would have been made easier by its removal. Meticulous masking with Fine Line tape around the edge of uneven emblems like this is difficult, especially if you do not want a trace of overspray to show. Most emblems of this type are attached with two pins secured by clips on the inside of the fender. Some exceptions are found where emblems are attached with two-way tape.

clear paint. If color actually rubs off, you have no clear coat paint present.

Body parts removal

A car's finish that calls for complete paint removal will also require the dismantling of all emblems, body-side molding, trim, light fixtures, bumpers and the like. This is so every spot of paint can be worked on and unnecessary damage to unpainted body parts will be prevented. Masking endeavors and paint coverage into tight spaces are much easier when obstructions are removed.

Part removal does not have to be a factor in every custom paint situation. If your car sports an existing paint job that is in good shape and the new design you plan to apply will only cover open body areas, there is no reason to take off unaffected emblems, trim or molding. However, if the pattern you plan to spray will encompass areas around emblems or trim, you should remove them in order to ensure excellent paint coverage. One tiny flaw in the masking of an emblem can throw off an entire custom paint scheme.

Door handles are loosened from inside the door. You will have to remove the inner door panel to allow access to the handle mechanism. Every latch mechanism is different, so take your time to determine just exactly how it all comes apart. Be sure to save all parts in a separate container, as losing any of them will cause problems during replacement. Empty coffee cans with plastic lids make ideal containers for small body parts, screws and washers.

Interior door panel removal procedures also vary with each auto make and model. Some are attached with screws, others utilize push-in clips to secure them to door frames. Some European models feature ribbed plastic pins which are pushed into mounting holes and held in place by finned appendages. Many times, once pins are forced out of their holes, they lose retention strength and have to be replaced. If you are unclear as to how the inner door panels are removed from your car, seek advice from related shop manuals, dealership service centers or professional autobody technicians.

Emblems and badges are attached to body panels with stems and clips, or screws and nuts. Carefully

Opening car doors into walls, posts and other cars sometimes causes small dents along door edges like this. Here, a door is held secure on one side while a block of wood is laid against the inside edge and then gently tapped with a hammer until a small dent is pushed out. A block of wood cushions hits from the hammer to prevent paint chips and also to spread the hammer's blows evenly along the dent to effect a smooth and even repair.

Bodyside molding is attached to this 1989 Chevrolet Astro Van by way of plastic clips. Each clip snaps onto a metal pin, shown here as a small circle located about ½ inch away from the upper left corner of the clip. The center of the clip fits over the pin, and rails featured at the top and bottom of molding pieces snap onto the clip.

investigate their mounting arrangements before pulling or prying on emblems or badges; unnecessary force could not only damage them, it could cause dents or wrinkles on surrounding body panel areas.

Many of the newer cars and trucks feature emblems, badges and trim that are attached by way of heavy-duty two-way tape. You can look on the inside edge of trunk lids to see if pins penetrate the sheet metal just behind emblems or nameplates. If none exist, that adornment is attached with two-way tape. For other items, like bodyside moldings, use your fingernail to gently pull trim away from the car body. Look closely at the space behind the trim to locate the attaching mechanism, be it tape, pins or clips.

Two-way tape is loosened in a couple of ways. You can purchase adhesive remover at the autobody paint and supply store or use heat from a hair blow dryer. Adhesive removers are solvent-based liquids designed to attack the adhesive power of tape. Be sure to read and follow all directions carefully. Electric blow

dryers work well to heat up adhesive tape and cause it to lose its bonding ability. Go slow and don't expect the process to work instantly. Gently pull up on the emblem or trimpiece while applying hot air to the backside area. As adhesive is loosened, the piece will pull further away from the car body.

Some clips are removed with simple pressure. Autobody technicians use small, wide-bladed plug pullers to slip behind clips; with just a little prying, clips quickly pop off. To protect the paint surface, a short section from a wooden paint stick is placed between the car body and plug puller.

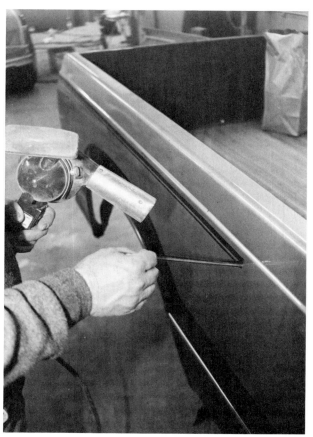

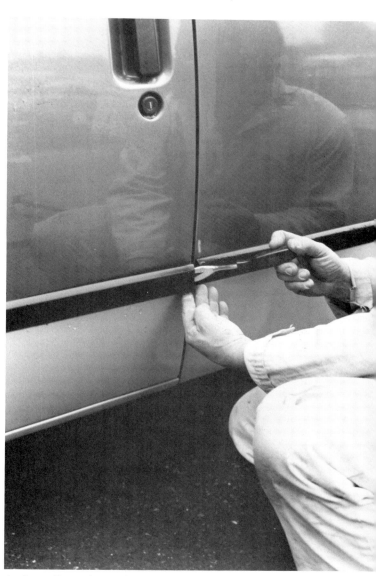

Using a heat gun to loosen adhesive, Laursen peels vinyl pinstripe tape from the bed of a Mazda sport truck. Hair blow dryers work just as well to gently release the grip of vinyl stripes and graphics. A great deal of heat is not needed; in fact, too much could blister paint and cause vinyl to stretch excessively and tear. Go slow. Apply heat just ahead of the part being pulled off. Too much heat is being applied if the surface gets too hot for you to comfortably handle it with a bare hand.

A plug puller tool is used to pop off bodyside molding from a 1989 Chevrolet Astro Van. Caution must be used in order to avoid chipping paint. In this case, the rear molding section is used as a base for the plug puller. In other cases, a thin piece of wood could be used under the tool to protect paint and spread out the amount of force being applied while the tool is used for leverage to pop clips loose.

A small bodyside molding pin was ground off leaving behind this bare metal scrape. About 1½ inches directly to the left of the grinding mark is a small circle denoting the location of another pin which will be ground off. Each grinding blemish will require filler material to be placed over it, then will be sanded with 360 to 400 grit sandpaper to fill in and hide deep grinding scratches.

If you cannot determine how to detach some items from the car body, confer with a service technician at a dealership or professional autobody paint shop. It would be much better to pay just a small fee for expert service, than to tug on and damage an emblem or trim, scratching or denting part of the car body during the process.

Paint stripping

Chemical paint strippers do a good job of loosening paint on car bodies. This process of paint removal is messy and you should be properly prepared. In order to reduce the mess, many professionals lay down a sheet of heavy-grade plastic under the car to extend past the outer vehicle edges before starting paint removal procedures. This way, paint residue is confined to the plastic and can be easily picked up and discarded when the job is done.

Chemicals used as paint strippers are potent. You must strictly follow label directions for application and

Newlook Autobody technician Mike Kane uses a welder with low amperage to fill in two holes left after the removal of an emblem from this 1989 Chevrolet Astro Van driver's door. Turning the welder on and off to keep heat as low as possible, Kane welds around the hole's circumference first to establish a solid surface onto which further beads will eventually cover the hole. The thin nature of new car sheet metal requires extremely light touches with welders to prevent metal fatigue, warping or other damage.

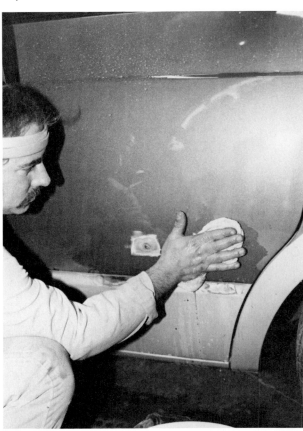

Kane applies a sopping wet towel of cool water to a door skin after completing a weld. He has found that this greatly helps to prevent sheet metal warping, especially on thin-skinned panels. Metal will be red hot right after welding, and you will have to be absolutely certain only the towel touches it. Kane keeps towels in a bucket of water next to his work area and pulls them out of the water wringing wet to be directly applied to metal. Heat expands and bulges metal while water helps to cool and shrink it back to shape.

Kane uses a grinder to smooth welds after filling holes left by emblems. Notice that he is wearing a full face shield; gloves and a filter mask should be considered for optimum safety performance. Sparks from grinding operations are plenty hot enough to set flammable liquids on fire. Be sure all paint products and thinners are located safely away from this kind of work.

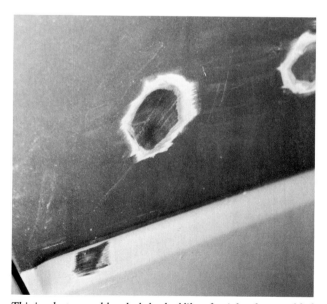

This is what an emblem hole looked like after it has been welded and smoothed with a grinder. Four separate shades of color are shown from the inside of the spot toward the outer circumference. Innermost, of course, is bare metal. The small ring next to bare metal is primer. Next, the lightest shade, is a base color coat used in combination with the actual color coat that is seen on the vehicle, the fourth and outermost color.

removal. Be sure to wear heavy-duty rubber gloves and use all other safety equipment advised by the product label.

Since removing paint with a chemical stripper requires scraping on a car body with a putty knife, you must be aware that severe scratching is a potential hazard. If the car body is in excellent shape and you just simply want to remove paint without having to do metal repair, you might want to consider an alternative method of paint removal.

For automobiles of classic vintage with flowing lines, near-perfect bodies and minimal paint thickness to remove, custom painters frequently opt to use a Dual Action power sander for paint stripping. This process

Kane mixes a batch of polyester filler and hardener on a piece of clean smooth plexiglass. This material will be applied to the repair work done on emblem holes to fill in grinder scratches and small imperfections left after welding. Be sure to follow filler and hardener instructions carefully in order to prepare workable mixtures that will adhere and perform as expected.

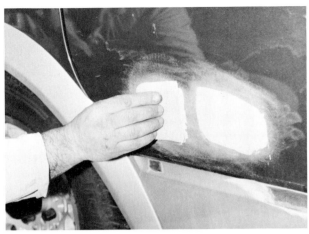

Using a plastic squeegee made for body filler application, Kane applies material over the entire work surface surrounding what used to be emblem holes. Although he will attempt to get filler on in a smooth and even application, sanding efforts will be required to totally smooth the repair before it is ready for primer and paint. Be sure to allow ample time for the material to cure before sanding.

Kane uses a Dual Action sander with 80 grit paper to initially smooth body filler cured over the old emblem holes. Coarse sandpaper makes quick work of reducing a rather rough filler surface to a smooth finish. This effort will be followed with additional sanding in order to effect a paintable surface finish. For maximum personal safety, he should have the face shield down and should be wearing gloves and a filter mask.

will take longer than a chemical one, but the results will be cleaner and worries about putty knife damage are gone.

A great deal of sanding dust will be encountered during such an operation. To protect items located in the engine compartment, tape a sheet of plastic over the top of the compartment just below the fenders. Additional plastic sheets can be attached easily to the outer edges of the underbody and then to the floor to prevent sanding dust from entering open areas about the undercarriage, like brake assemblies, exhaust pipes, U-joints and engine assemblies.

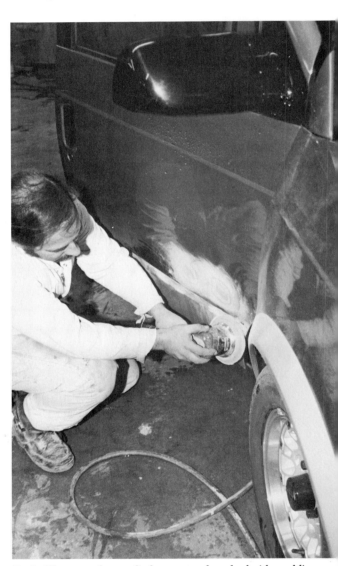

Body filler was also applied to spots where bodyside molding pins were ground off. Here, Kane uses a Dual Action sander to smooth them. When sanding efforts have been completed with 80 grit paper, 100 grit is used for further smoothing to get material even with the surrounding body surface. Final sanding is done with a hand-held sanding block and 600 grit paper. Kane has opened the door to allow clean sanding and maneuverability at this door edge next to the fender flare.

Seams around the hood, trunk and doors should be sealed with 2 inch tape. This maneuver will help to prevent large dust accumulations from entering the passenger compartment, engine and trunk spaces. Not only will it make future cleaning a bit easier, it will also eliminate a lot of unnecessary sanding dust from entering the spray booth at painting time. Remove tape after the majority of sanding has been completed in order to reach paint that had been covered by it.

Sandblasters offer another means by which to remove paint from car bodies. Paint can be removed from many cars in less than two hours by sandblasting. The process is simple, as long as prescribed precautions are followed. By far, the most critical factors in sandblasting are related to the media and pressures employed. Media comes in a number of different grades and materials. Harsh media and high pressure can quickly warp panels, especially on newer vehicles that feature thin sheet metal panels.

Sandblasters can be purchased through autobody supply stores, tool outlets and mail-order businesses like Eastwood. Eastwood carries different sandblasting models, complete with fittings and nozzles. You can also rent sandblasters at rental yards.

The media used to remove paint from cars is an important consideration. Silica-type abrasives have been known to cause respiratory problems, and users are advised to wear respiratory protection. You must also wear heavy-duty gloves and a sandblasting hood when performing this type of work. Plastic media, like ground up buttons, has been found to do a good job of paint stripping. Other types of abrasives have also worked well for custom painters when used at appropriate pressures. Charts and instructional pamphlets accompany many new sandblasting outfits and are also available at many autobody supply stores and facilities that sell sandblasting equipment and abrasives.

Sanding

If your car has undergone some body repair, you have to use a coarse sandpaper to smooth out and shape body filler. When the proper contour has been achieved with 100 or 150 grit paper, further smoothing is accomplished using 400 to 500 grit paper. This will

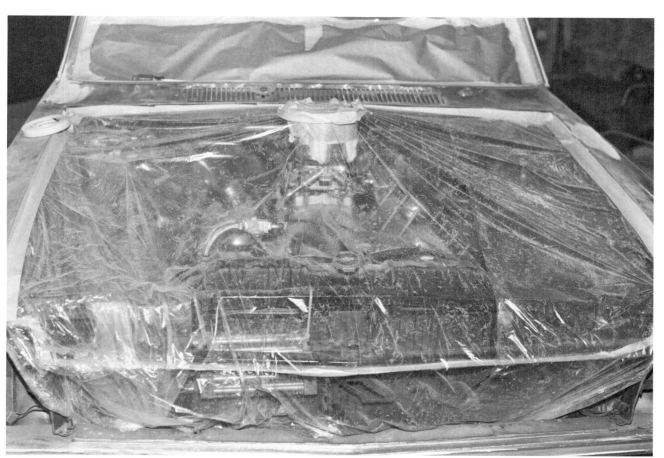

This high-performance 1965 Chevy II is scheduled for a complete repaint. Old paint was removed by sanding and sandblasting. Because a great deal of sanding dust and sandblasting media would be encountered, the engine compartment was covered with thick plastic. Covering engine compartments and sealing off other areas with plastic and tape protects uninvolved car assemblies and prevents dust from accumulating in hidden areas, an important factor to consider before rolling a vehicle into a paint booth.

Plastic has been laid over the roof structure of this Jeep to protect it from dust during sanding and sandblasting operations. Plastic should fare well as a guard against light overspray during small custom paint endeavors but should not be expected to protect against overspray when completing a full body paint job. When a major part of a car body is to be painted, use auto masking paper to protect uninvolved surfaces.

Mycon will use this Eastwood sandblaster to remove scale and other surface imperfections from under the bumper area on this 1965 Chevy II. When used according to directions and with the correct media and pressure combinations, sandblasters can make short work of many surface preparation jobs. Note the heavy-duty sandblasting hood, gloves and respirator Mycon will wear while sandblasting.

remove sanding scratches left behind by the coarser paper, yet leave the surface just rough enough to provide a bonding surface for new paint.

Mycon uses 600 grit sandpaper to roughen up finishes on paint jobs in preparation for the application of new custom paint. This roughing-up process is important when preparing a newer, baked-on factory paint surface for the addition of custom paint products.

Whenever you rub on a body surface with sandpaper, always use some kind of a paint block. This will guarantee that your smoothing efforts will be uniform, flat and even. In tight spots, be creative. Mycon commonly uses the end of a wooden paint stir stick as a sanding block to reach into tight spaces and along contours too narrow for conventional blocks.

As you sand, occasionally feel the sanded surface with your free hand. Note irregularities, bumps and rough textures. Concentrate sanding efforts on those problems but be sure to sand more than just one spot. Feather out your sanding perimeter to include about two to three times the rough area in need of actual

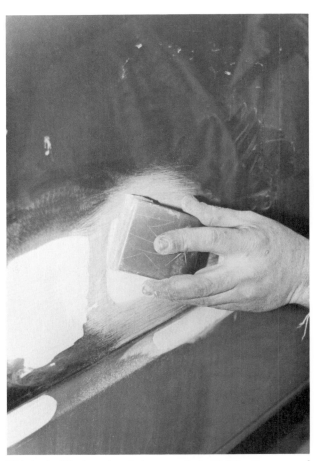

This body filler has already been sanded with 80 grit paper and a Dual Action sander. In order to obtain a smoother surface, Kane uses 100 grit paper and a hand-held sanding block to reduce ridges, bumps and other imperfections. Sanding by hand without the use of a block would result in an uneven surface finish. If a lot of dust is expected, a filter mask should be worn.

sanding. Graduate to higher-grade sandpaper as surfaces become more smooth and in line with contours and body shape. Using 500 to 600 grit paper will remove harsh sanding scratches left by coarser paper and should leave the surface smooth enough for paint.

Before spraying primer or paint, always wipe off surfaces with a tack rag. These special cloths are designed to pick up minute bits of dust, lint and debris. They will leave surfaces debris free and ready for spraying.

Priming

In most cases, there is no need to use primer when applying custom paint over an existing, factory-baked paint job. However, you should lightly sand this kind of surface with 400 to 600 grit paper, clean it according to the new paint's instructions and then spray on an adhesion promoter. You should be aware that some paint manufacturers may refer to their adhesion promoters as primer-sealers.

Adhesion promoters help new paint bond to surfaces already painted. In the case of factory baked-on finishes, the surface is so hard that new paint may not bond at all. Laursen is a firm believer in adhesion promoters and recommends their use over every factory baked-on paint finish prior to the application of custom paint finishes.

Undercoats are those products applied to a car body surface before the application of paint. On bare metal, you must first apply primer before considering paint. The primer's first job is to promote adhesion between the paint and the metal. In addition to that, primers like PPG's DP 40 will inhibit rust.

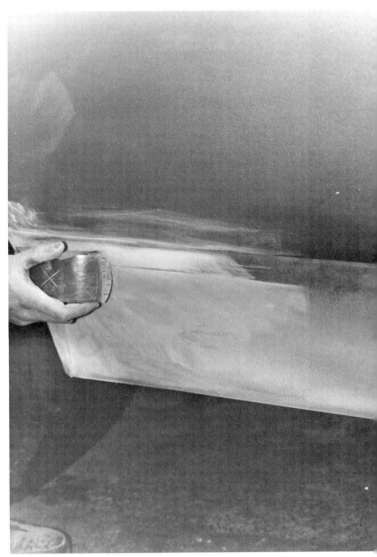

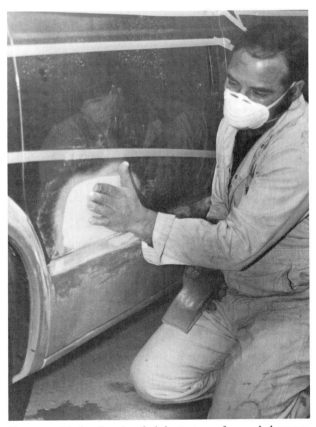

Kane uses his free hand to feel the texture of a sanded area to determine if more sanding is needed. This is common practice and one that can be learned quite quickly. If the surface does not feel smooth and even, it will not look smooth even after it is painted. Sanding is time-consuming work and critical to the final visual outcome of any custom paint job. Notice that Kane is wearing a filter mask during sanding operations.

Kane's thumb and the front left corner of the sanding block are located inside a grooved section featured on the lower panel of a 1989 Chevrolet Astro Van. Bodyside molding clip pins were ground off this section. In the middle of the picture at the far right side, you will notice a spotted surface appearance, the effect made by the application of a guide coat. This primer-surfacer material sprays on in a combination of light and dark colors to assist sanding by showing low (dark) spots. When the surface displays a solid color, it has been smoothed flat.

67

Apply primer according to the label instructions and information on its product sheet. The best type of primer to use over bare metal is epoxy primer. This product requires use of a catalyst, which is mixed in at the time of application. Two coats are generally recommended.

After bare metal has been coated with a rust-inhibiting primer, consideration must be given to the smoothness of the surface. To fill in minor flaws like grinder or sander scratches, a primer-surfacer is applied. Loaded with much more solids than plain primer, a primer-surfacer fills in low spots and at the same time makes high spots higher. This is when you will need to block sand with 360 to 500 grit sandpaper. As the high spots are knocked down, low spots will remain untouched for the most part, therefore making the surface flat and smooth.

Two to three coats of primer-surfacer are commonly suggested. Make sure the product is thoroughly mixed before adding a thinner solvent. This is to guar-

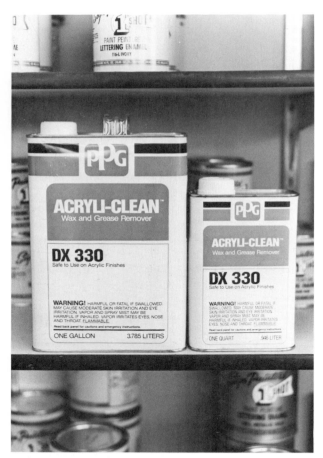

Before any material is sprayed on body surfaces, they must be cleaned with wax and grease remover. All paint manufacturers either produce their own brand of wax and grease remover or recommend a specific brand to be used with their paint system. PPG's Acryli-Clean is safe to use on all acrylic finishes. Be sure to follow application directions, including the use of rubber gloves.

antee that all solids are evenly mixed into the entire can of material. It is important to wait the appropriate amount of time between coats in order to allow solvents to evaporate; these are called flash times. If additional coats are applied too soon, solvents trapped in previous coats will cause shrinkage of the material into grinding or sanding scratches which will show up later through primer-surfacer and paint.

Additionally, sanding primer-surfacer too soon will also cause sanding scratches to show through. It is best you wait to sand primer-surfacer until it has dried completely, generally at least one hour. Always follow the instructions listed on primer-surfacer labels and on their information sheets.

Primer-sealers are products designed to protect an underlying paint from a different type that is going to be applied over it, such as lacquer over enamel. This is important for custom painters who plan to apply a lacquer-based graphic or other design over an enamel paint job.

There are other uses for primer-sealers, such as preventing the solvents of a new paint from penetrating the surface of a primer-surfacer. Solvent penetration of this kind may induce sand scratch swelling to make the surface appear rough. Use of a primer-sealer depends on the type of paint on your car and the type of paint you want to put on top of it. It is best in all cases to confer with your autobody paint and supply jobber. For each individual situation, that person should be able to advise which applications require primer-sealer.

Wax and grease removal

Perhaps the most commonly used product in any professional autobody paint shop is wax and grease remover. Nothing can ruin a custom paint job faster than contaminants on the surface to be painted. Without a clean painting surface, bubbles, fisheyes and a number of other flaws will appear almost immediately.

Wax and grease remover products are mild solvents. They are poured onto clean soft cloths and then wiped onto a car's body. Mycon likes to make a few passes with a cloth soaked in wax and grease remover first and then follow up with a clean dry cloth.

After your car has been thoroughly washed and dried, it is a good idea to clean it again with wax and grease remover. To further ensure the surface is really clean, wipe it off again with wax and grease remover after masking has been completed and you are ready for paint.

Glass cleaner

Laursen also has had great results cleaning car finishes with an aerosol glass cleaner after using wax and grease remover. Ammonia in these types of glass cleaners helps pick up remnants of silicone products and also helps to reduce moisture on the vehicle surface. They dry quickly and leave behind a super clean surface.

Roy Dunn, the pinstriper, uses aerosol glass cleaner with ammonia to reduce static electricity on fiberglass panels he pinstripes. Static electricity makes hairs on his brushes stick out which then cause paint splotches alongside pinstripes.

If you have used silicone-based multipurpose dressings on the interior of your car or on vinyl and rubber parts on the exterior, you should use an ammonia-based glass cleaner as a final cleaning agent before painting. Even if you only used silicone dressing on your car's interior, those silicone agents may have rubbed off of seats and surrounding parts to infiltrate your clothes. Just leaning against your car could have transferred them from your clothes to the car's exterior body finish.

Silicone problems

Car paint protectants that are supposed to last for a year, even through the most harsh weather conditions, are usually loaded with silicone additives. Laursen says that some of these so-called miracle paint preservatives are so filled with silicone products that silicone agents filter through paint right down to bare metal.

In these special cases, you can try a fisheye eliminator product. Chances are you will have to strip paint to bare metal, then clean the metal over and over again to remove all traces of silicone. If you don't, paint will fisheye everywhere and will not bond like it is supposed to.

Poly-glycoats and other such finish protectors rely on silicones to ward off the effects of sun rays and other climatic conditions. They work well, especially when rejuvenated every six months as directed, but repainting those surfaces can be quite a problem.

Fiberglass preparation

Painted fiberglass panels do not present much of a problem with repainting or in applying new graphic designs. New fiberglass does pose problems in that materials on a new surface could cause serious fisheye blemishes. This is because mold-release materials have not been thoroughly removed from the body surface.

Extra attention should be given new fiberglass pieces in wax and grease cleaning. Sanding alone will not remove these agents; in fact, sanding will simply cause them to be engrained into the surface even deeper.

After cleaning, apply a coat of epoxy primer. This is not to prevent rust, but rather to promote better adhesion of subsequent coats of base and color paint. After that, most custom painters apply an adhesion promoter to guarantee good paint bonding. If this process does not work successfully, you will have to use a fisheye eliminating product.

Laursen prefers to follow wax and grease remover cleaning with an application of aerosol glass cleaner before painting. He feels that the ammonia in this type of product helps to remove any lingering traces of silicone and also assists in drying body sur- *faces. Dunn regards glass cleaner or rubbing alcohol usage as an absolute requirement when painting over plastic and fiberglass pieces to prevent static electricity from making the bristles on his paintbrush spring out wildly.*

7

Masking Techniques

The original purpose behind automotive paint masking was preventing spray paint from getting onto specific unpainted car parts. As time went on, car enthusiasts became more inventive, and soon many began to realize that masking could take on an entirely new dimension. Instead of painting car bodies one solid color, they could put on two colors thus creating two-tone models.

Eventually, bold painters started experimenting with various masking designs and color blends. They

This 1990 Chevrolet Suburban came from the factory a solid dark brown. The four lines you see running horizontally from the headlights were created by laying Fine Line tape down on top of the dark brown and then painting a lighter color over the top. When tape was pulled, dark lines were exposed. In this case, before Fine Line tape was pulled, the new light tinted paint was masked off and a contrasting shade was painted between the sets of dark lines. The combination of dark thin lines and wider colored lines offered an otherwise dull two-tone paint scheme a fresh appearance.

The factory color on this 1990 Chevrolet van is featured inside the thin lines outlining the light-colored graphic. After the light color had cured, a color just a few shades lighter than the factory color was sprayed over the outer edges of the graphic to create a new wider outline. That new color was also used to completely cover the top right section of the van which left behind a thin outline exposing the factory color.

came up with flames, scallops, racing stripes and a host of other patterns. By the 1960s, almost anything was acceptable, including wild murals of desert scenes, moonscapes and whatever else a customizer could imagine.

Custom paint designs are achieved through meticulous masking endeavors. The application of paint is easy in comparison. Plenty of forethought must go into a project before actual masking begins. Your masked patterns and coverage must be perfect, or else the entire job will look awkward, sloppy and unprofessional. You may find that masking takes a lot more time than anticipated, not only because it is intricate work, but also because setting tape down in just the perfect pattern isn't always possible on the first try.

Along with plenty of Fine Line and ¾ inch masking tape, have a couple of brand-new razor blades or X-acto knife blades on hand. A sharp blade will be needed to cut tape edges during various stages of the masking process.

Creating a design

Any kind of custom design can be created with the use of masking tape and paint. By practicing on an old hood or trunk lid, you can learn what works and what doesn't. That is exactly how original customizers learned their new-found craft.

Color schemes are important. If an assortment of colors does not blend well together, chances are that the overall custom effect will not be appreciated. On the other hand, subtle color blending can go a long way to make a certain design appear unique and truly custom.

Masking is just as important as color. A sloppy masking job will make brilliant colors just sit around as if they were thrown on with a paintbrush. If you are completely undecided on how a design will look on your car, take a few pictures of it from different angles. Have those pictures blown up to 8x10 inch size. Then use tracing paper and a soft pencil to trace the outline of the vehicle. Have a number of tracings copied and use those to draw in various custom graphics and other designs.

Use colored pencils or markers to fill in where you think they will look best. Keep practicing until you discover just the right pattern or design for your car. Tape that tracing to your car as you begin the masking

Accurately masking small items can be an intricate and time-consuming endeavor. Laursen makes the job of masking the door handles on Mycon's 1989 Chevrolet Astro Van a little easier by using a stool on wheels. The immediate area around these door handles will be painted with clear only. If a new color was planned, instead of just clear, the door handles and key lock would have been removed.

Innovative auto enthusiasts experimented with masking tape and paint to come up with unique custom paint designs. Flames, a favorite pattern for many car buffs, can be arranged in all kinds of different shapes, widths, lengths and colors, as these pink flames over a dark blue convertible body indicate. Continued experimentation led custom car painters in all sorts of directions, enabling them to effect myriad custom paint schemes, patterns and hues. Dan Mycon

In order to lay Fine Line tape on the edge of the door handle assembly, Laursen carefully uses the blade of a small pocket knife to hold tape in place. This effort will not afford a perfect masking job. However, since clear paint is the only product that will be sprayed over the area, signs of overspray will not be visible. If a new color were to be added inside the handle pocket, though, overspray would be plainly visible and make the job look sloppy. In that case, the handles should be removed.

Fine Line Tape or 1/8 inch paper tape may be needed to make the first masking line around an odd-shaped or small obstruction. When the thin tape has been accurately placed, wider tape can be easily attached to it in order to complete a masking endeavor. Using 3/4 inch tape to initially mask an unusually shaped part is difficult because of the tape's width and bulk size.

process. Time and again, you will look at it to help you keep the masking process going. If actual masking efforts do not turn out quite as nice as you envisioned, change them until you come up with what you want.

Once paint is on your car, you are more or less stuck with it until you decide to repaint. Mycon figures most people leave their custom paint schemes in place for at least five years. The time to change or rearrange patterns is while masking, not after the paint has been sprayed on.

Masking a design

Custom paint schemes that feature a lot of curves, arcs and points, like flames, are not easy to mask out on the first try. For those kinds of free-flowing jobs, many custom painters prefer to draw patterns on a car's sur-

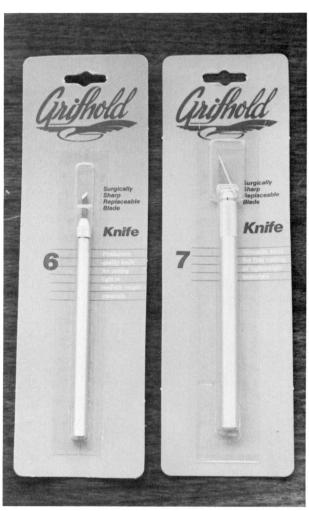

Sharp X-acto knives or razor blades will be needed to cut masking tape in certain circumstances, like trimming tape from the inside of intersecting patterns, for instance. Attempts to cut paper or plastic masking tape with a dull blade will result in tearing or pulling the tape away from the surface. Sharp blades do not require much pressure, and care should be taken not to cut through paint.

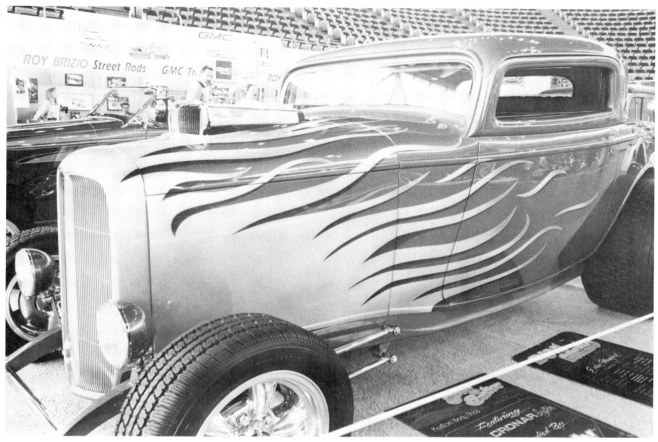

This flame design almost takes on a type of scallop approach. Instead of masking common flames, the custom painter gave each lick more of a straight shape and accented each one with a dark color. This is what is meant by imagination. One would have to surmise that the designer of this custom paint effort spent a lot of time contemplating its creation and even more time drawing or taping until the final outcome was met with approval.

Masking efforts for this drip design included the grille and front bumper. Although airbrush highlighting could cover some flaws in masking like sharp bends, it cannot totally make up for a sloppy job. In this case, time was taken to effect a unique front-end pattern that encompassed lining up the headlight assembly with the bumper. Steve Brown

face first and then use those lines as masking guidelines. It is far easier to apply masking tape along a line than it is to create your design while actually masking at the same time.

China Markers work well for outlining designs on car finishes, black markers are best suited for light-colored paint finishes and white markers for darker ones. The light lines made by these markers are easy to erase with a soft cloth. You can draw a design, erase it, draw another and erase it, and so on, until you come up with the perfect outline of what you had envisioned all along.

When the design has been drawn to your satisfaction, apply thin Fine Line tape around the outside edge of China Marker lines. This will ensure that the painted design will be as wide as desired. Many times, novice custom painters form their patterns a bit too narrow, and when tape is placed on the inside edge of the marker lines, the pattern becomes even more narrow. Don't worry about actual masking at this point. The purpose of Fine Line tape is to make an actual custom paint design edge and serve as a base for following applications of masking tape and paper.

Tape placement for flames will present this kind of problem, especially when masking tips. Tips are critical; flow to make the flames look alive. If they stood alone with no uniform pattern, the entire design could be off-balance and look awkward.

Custom paint schemes utilizing straight lines with gradual curves are easier to lay out with tape than attempting to draw with China Markers. To place tape in a long straight line along a car body, attach it first to a part of the body just ahead of where you want the

The splash design on Wingert's sport truck encompassed the doorjambs to finish off its custom paint scheme. The extra effort required more time, but since Wingert plans to keep the design in place for a long time, it was worth it. If you notice a flaw or oversight in your masking job, take the time necessary to repair or develop a new design before painting begins. An extra hour or even a few extra days taken to really perfect a masking job can make a great deal of difference in an overall custom paint job.

To help design intricate patterns, like flames, many custom painters prefer to draw designs on the car surface before applying tape. In those cases, China Markers work well. The soft material used to make marks will not scratch paint and is easily removed with wax and grease remover. On light-colored cars, use the dark marker. A white marker works best on dark surfaces.

design to start. Holding it away from the surface a few inches, stretch it out to the opposite end of the vehicle. Kneel down so that your eye is in line with the tape. Then, while carefully looking to see that the tape is still straight, slowly move it closer to the car body until it touches. Press that end against the body so that it stays in place.

Step back and look at the tape from different angles to be sure it is on straight. If it is placed just the way you want it, run your hand down its entire length to make sure every inch is firmly attached. Should it be crooked or placed incorrectly, pull it off from the back and while stretching it toward the back of the car to keep it taut, pull it away from the body so that all the tape comes off except the very front portion that was attached first. Then, try the same maneuver again.

It may take two or three tries before you get tape situated just the way you want it, so have patience. If that piece of tape begins to lose its adhesive strength, wad it up and throw it away. Start again with a new section.

Designing as you go

More often than not, custom painters start out with a specific design plan but find themselves moving tape

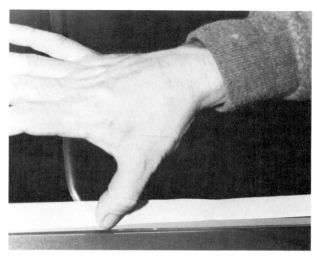

The ¾ inch paper masking tape is applied on top of Fine Line tape. To effect a perfect masking job next to window trim molding, Laursen used Fine Line tape. The thin nature of Fine Line made it easy to apply tape along the thin molding strip edge. This application of ¾ inch tape will be used as a wide base for the application of paper and tape, the next step in this masking process.

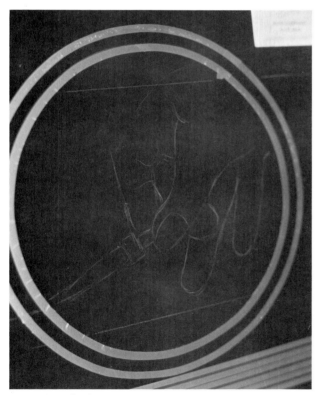

Dunn drew freehand this design of a hand holding a pinstripe brush on the side of his 1935 Chevrolet panel truck. Since the vehicle is black, he used a white China Marker. Mistakes made during the process were quickly erased using a soft cloth. The taped circle surrounding the drawing was outlined with the marker by tracing a paint can lid. It took a few tries to get Fine Line tape to lay down perfectly along the line.

The application of tape for flame designs should be free flowing with no sharp bends, like the one in the middle of the second-to-last taped line. This takes practice and a lot of it. The hand that holds the roll of tape will be raised and lowered as the pattern demands. The free hand will follow closely behind to actually push tape against the surface to effect the design. If you have never designed flames before, practice with a China Marker and make sure you have three or four rolls of Fine Line tape on hand.

around to create an even better effect. As they come to a curve, point or other break, they move the tape millimeters at a time until they discover just the right eye-appealing dimension.

While setting up a graphics design on Mycon's van, Mycon and Caldwell spent over two hours perfecting just the right shape for a point pattern on the left rear door. First it was too narrow, then too wide, then too long, short and off-center. Considering all of the features of the entire rear section of the van, they finally found a pattern that blended well and was geometrically pleasing to the eye.

Until tape is actually on a car body, it is difficult to envision what a certain custom design will look like. You can mask off major areas with little problem but may find that perfecting little curves, arcs, points and angles can be perplexing. Take your time and don't settle for anything less than what you had hoped for.

If you have never applied a custom design to a car before, make sure you have extra rolls of Fine Line tape on hand. Chances are you might go through a roll or two while moving lines and patterns around in search of that perfect configuration.

Maintaining even dimensions

If points, bands and other straight designs are not evenly spaced or placed in some kind of visually rhythmic pattern, an entire scheme can be thrown off-balance. When masking scallops, graphics, stripes and other such arrangements, consider using a ruler or tape measure to map out locations where points stop or the specific widths of separate color bands or graphics.

Use a China Marker to pinpoint measured spots where lines of tape should intersect to form a point or to designate the specific widths of various color bands. If items are supposed to be offset, use a measuring device to make sure they are offset at equally spaced intervals.

To lay a straight line of tape, Mycon attached it to a predetermined starting point on the rear taillight and then stretched the tape taut while walking toward the front of the van. As he neared his mark at the door, he squatted down so his eye was level with tape and then carefully moved it to the mark. Once the tape was in place, he stood back to make sure it looked right. If it had not been placed correctly, he would have removed it and repeated the procedure.

Laying down a long straight line of tape will require that you check it after each application to be sure it is straight. To make it a bit easier to pick up and reposition the tape and to help preserve the amount of tape used, you can simply hang the roll as shown here.

This will give the job a sense of uniformity and offer a pleasant visual perception instead of throwing everything off-balance.

A tape measure or ruler can also help you to maintain identical lines or patterns that match on both sides of a vehicle. For horizontal spacing, measure from a point on the front fender back to a specific location under the corner of the rear side window. That same measurement can be graphed on the other side by using the same points featured on that side.

For example, let's say you want to paint a wide band of different colors down the side of your sport truck. At specific intervals, you want to include a heartbeat pattern. Although people really can't see both sides of the truck at the same time, you still want the lines to look the same on each side. The graphic should be placed down from the window line the same distance on both sides, and spacing for the heartbeats should be equal.

Determine certain landmarks that are featured equally on both sides of the vehicle, such as signal light trim corners, windshield corners, door handles, key holes or fender ridges. If the band will run from the headlights to the taillights, for instance, pick a certain spot on the front of the vehicle, like a signal light, and run a straight line of tape from it to a specific point near the back, like a spot on the taillight lens. Measure the distance from the top of the front and back light fixtures to the top of the tape. Measure that same distance on the lights located on the other side of the truck. These will denote where tape is to be placed on that side.

For the heartbeats, measure from a door or panel edge along the tape line to the spot where you want the design to start. Then, from that starting point, determine how long it will be—let's say 1 foot. On the other side, make the same measurements from the same landmarks located on that side.

Your graphics band should be equally wide on both sides of the vehicle and located the same distance from the window line. Heartbeats will be positioned the same distance from an edge of a door or panel and will be identical in length. To make sure the height and depth of the heartbeats are the same, simply measure

Mycon placed a line of ¾ inch masking tape close to where he felt the final graphic pattern would be located. This showed Kane just how far he could go with filling and sanding efforts while working to fill and smooth holes left by emblem and molding clip pin removal. The area above the tape will remain

untouched, and he didn't want to have to touch up paint that was already in fine shape. At the back of the van, Mycon is playing with tape to get an idea of what his designed arc-and-point graphic will look like.

Unless you have a lot of experience in the custom paint field, visualizing a completed custom paint design is difficult without an aid. About the easiest visual aid to employ is a practice session with a roll or two of tape. In this case, Fine Line tape is used to begin an eventual flame pattern. Tape will be placed near this point and then removed a number of times until its shape meets with the applicator's approval.

The hand holding the roll of tape actually moves in all directions according to how the design is to be outlined. The other hand holds tape in place and slides along to make sure it is attached to the surface. This takes a bit of coordination between your eyes and both hands. The best way to make a design is with plenty of patience and practice.

down from a point on the window line to where you want the top to apex; do the same for the bottom.

Checkerboard patterns, graphics and all symmetrical custom paint designs are laid out much the same way. You can even start out with just one strategically placed line of tape and make marks on it to determine intersections for other lines or places where special colors will be sprayed. You must remember, though, marks made on tape will be covered over after paint has been applied. If you will need to use certain marks for masking effort locations for additional color applications, simply cover them with small pieces of tape before spraying paint.

Practice makes perfect

Making a piece of tape lay down just the way you want it to is not as easy as it may sound. Straight lines are simple enough, but what about curves?

Custom painters generally lay out their designs by holding a roll of Fine Line in one hand and forming the

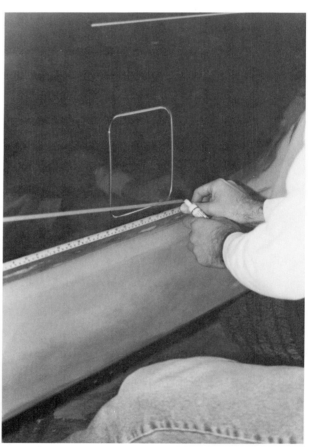

In order for this graphic design to feature points at the same spot on both sides of the van, Mycon uses a tape measure to mark specific tape application locations. He will use a starting point that is common to both sides of the van, for example, the bottom of the parking light assembly. At certain measured increments, marks are made to indicate where tape should be placed. This can be done at the start of the project, or an entire side can be masked first and then measurements taken and duplicated on the other side.

design with the other. A right-handed painter will attach the end of a tape roll to a point where the design starts. Tape will be stretched out about two to three feet and held taut with the roll remaining in the painter's right hand. As he or she moves the roll up or down to create a curve, the left hand slides up the length of tape to secure it in place. Should the placement not look right, tape is pulled away and started again.

Before tackling a unique custom design, use a roll of tape to practice with. Try different patterns, curves and bends. You will notice that paper tape folds and twists when you attempt to make it go in a curved pattern. For those movements, use Fine Line plastic tape. It stretches to make forming rounded edges much easier, smoother and less time consuming.

Tape-paint designs

If you want the color of your car to show through a custom paint design, all you have to do is cover sections of it with masking tape. For instance, let's say you want to create a design on the hood scoop of your car. It is currently red and you want some of the red to show through a black color you plan to paint over it.

Simply lay down tape of the width and pattern you desire and paint over it. When the paint is dry, gently pull off tape and your design will show.

Custom painters have had a lot of fun with this sort of technique. You can create some elaborate schemes by painting the base in a hodgepodge of different colors all running together. When the paint has dried, lay a pattern of Fine Line or other thin tape over it in any design you desire. Then cover it all with whatever color you are painting the entire panel. When that dries, pull off the tape to reveal a unique pattern of various colors.

The same type of thing can be done using a number of different colors and tape patterns. First, lay down a

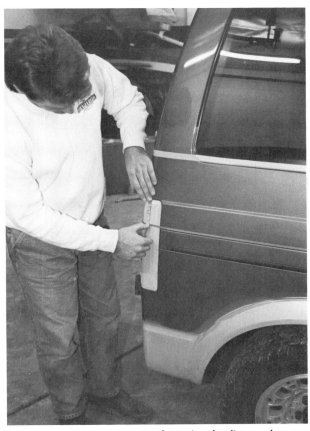

Mycon uses a tape measure to determine the distance between the top edge of tape and the top edge of the taillight assembly to make sure it matches with the measurement on the other side. This kind of meticulous masking effort makes the difference between a good custom paint job and a great one.

Splash designs do not normally require identical patterns for each side of a vehicle. However, should you want small areas like this to be identical, you can use measurements to mark the lowest spots and highest spots of the design. In this case, the highest part of the light-colored arc will be just below the rear edge of the reflector by so many inches and the point at which the design starts on the fenderwell lip is so many inches up from the ground.

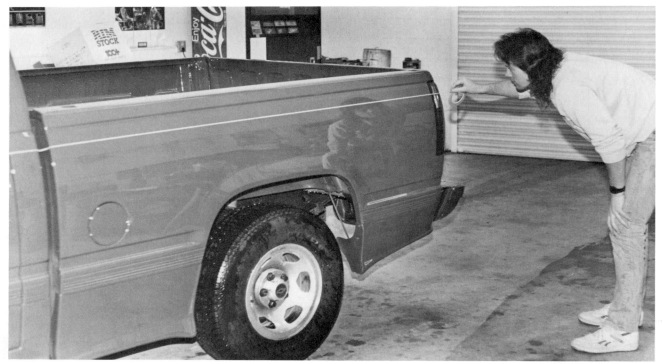

Having placed Fine Line tape in a straight line along the side of this 1990 Chevrolet sport truck, Dunn carefully continues to place tape around the taillight lens. It will take a few tries before tape goes around the fixture at just the right plane. Once it has

been secured around the lens, he will stretch the tape taut and then lay it across the tailgate in one motion, making sure it is placed at exactly the same spot on the opposite taillight as this one.

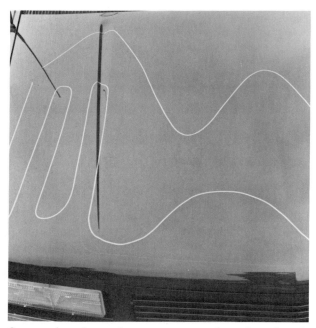

Once you learn how to lay tape on a car surface, about the only way to perfect your abilities is with practice. It may look easy to apply symmetrical scallops, but it is not. You have to have a balance point where points stop, and each scallop should be equidistant from the other. Even laying down a line for the splash look will not be accomplished on the first try. It just takes practice to make smooth flowing lines.

pattern of tape in a series of straight lines and rounded corners. Then spray on a certain color. When the paint has dried, apply another line of tape in the same fashion as the first but not exactly following the same lines. Follow that with another coat of different colored paint. When dry, pull the tape and check out the design.

Some custom painters call this the endless line design. As more tape and color are added, the design takes on more of a colorful and unique appearance. You can overdo this, however, and should be aware that too much paint on a surface is not good.

Special masking techniques

Airbrush artists have employed a number of various masking techniques to create truly custom paint designs on everything from cars and trucks to vans and motorcycle tanks. Ribbons, interwoven lines, fish scales and card patterns are just a few.

Stencils are widely used by artists to airbrush landscape and seascape scenes on the sides of vans and tailgates of pickup trucks. You can make your own stencils by cutting out pictures from magazines. Use cut-outs to make an outline by taping them to a surface and painting over them. You could also cut a picture out and tape the page to a surface in order to paint the full picture.

The theory of masking is simple: just cover whatever it is you don't want painted. Conversely, if you want a particular spot covered in a certain color, leave it exposed. Practice is the key. Do not expect to lay out a perfect pattern on the first try. Plan plenty of time to determine how the pattern is effected and then allot enough time to put it in place.

Masking for overspray protection

Especially for full paint jobs, a number of items either have to be removed from a vehicle or adequately masked before painting begins. These include outer door mirrors, door handles, trim, emblems, badges, bumpers and lights. Professional autobody paint shops almost always remove parts in lieu of masking. The reason is that unless masking is perfect, tiny overspray blotches will show.

One would not be expected to strip an entire car body just to put on a few color stripes, heartbeats or freak drops. However, if you plan to paint all of the body except the roof, you must seriously consider part removal. If areas around door handles and window trim will simply be coated with clear after some color graphics have been applied to the side body, you can easily get away with just masking. You must be certain that all parts of the obstructions are completely covered with tape and that tape does not extend to the body. This is a meticulous process.

The first step in masking an item is to cover its outer edge. This is the most critical. On small items, use tape of a workable width—¾ inch as opposed to 2 inch. Carefully lay tape along the object's edge without extending it onto the painted surface. Go around the entire circumference. Then fold the tape down on top of the item. If the object is small, cover it up completely with strips of tape.

Articles of awkward dimension, like lights, can be fully covered with tape to save the hassle of folding and cutting paper to fit. Overlap the tape by at least ½ inch. This will ensure paint does not bleed through seams.

Larger items, like windows, should have their edges masked with tape first to ensure they are adequately covered and that masking does not cover any painted surface. When that has been done, cover the rest of the glass with paper secured by tape. Be sure to run a line of tape down all seams. If this is not done, air pressure from the paint gun can force seams open and overspray will infiltrate the area.

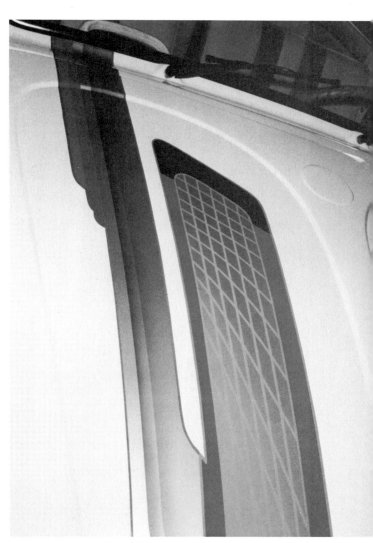

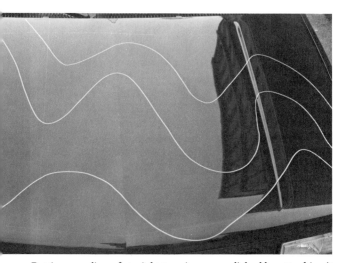

Putting on a line of straight tape is accomplished by attaching it to one point and stretching it to another. For all intents and purposes, the tape stays straight for you. On the other hand, curves require a steady hand and excellent hand-to-eye coordination, even if you just simply want to follow another line. For designs incorporating wavy lines or lots of curves, novice custom painters are much better off drawing their designs first with a China Marker and then following with tape.

Although there are no less than nine colors in this design, masking efforts were not that difficult to employ. Note that most of the lines are straight, even though plenty of forethought was given to exact measurements and even spacing. A few simple rounded corners have been employed but only those outlining the graphic on the right were required to be identical. This graphic is appealing and could be easily duplicated by anyone who spends enough time developing a systematic plan for its application. Steve Brown

81

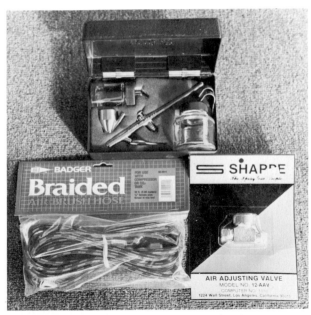

This Badger airbrush system includes airbrush, paint cups, spray tips and hose. Murdock recommends users also consider the use of an air adjusting valve to help further control delicate paint patterns. A tool like this is useful for a number of various applications during custom painting. Besides highlighting drip and splash effects, airbrushes can be used to blend different colors on small designs or accents.

All masking will not be within easy reach. Here, Laursen applies masking tape to sections exposed by removal of the front bumper. Since it was easiest to reach those spots while laying on the floor, he used a wide sheet of masking paper as a mat to keep his clothes clean. A short section of carpet may have been a little more comfortable.

A section of an arc-and-point graphic design will go across the gasoline tank filler door. To prevent overspray from spoiling the jamb area for the door, Mycon applies masking tape along its edge. To make working on this rather low item a bit easier, he uses a milk crate for a stool. Notice that the seams for masking paper covering the windows are sealed with tape. This is to prevent air pressure from the spray paint gun from blowing the seams open to make glass vulnerable to overspray.

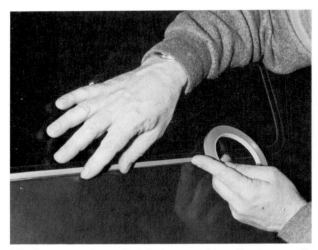

The first tape to be applied during a masking effort is generally the piece that covers the most outer edge of the obstruction. Laursen is using Fine Line tape to make a tight masking job along the bottom edge on a section of window trim. The hand holding the roll of tape must guide the tape close to its intended position, while the other hand makes sure the tape gets adequately secured.

To ensure overspray does not mar door jambs, thoroughly mask them. Use 2 inch tape to cover all parts of door jambs to their outermost part. If needed, use paper to cover all metal surfaces. Be sure to secure tape to weather stripping so it does not get covered with paint.

Most auto painters try to seal gaps between door edges and jambs with 2 inch tape. This is to prevent overspray from landing on jamb pieces. You can do this by opening the door and fastening tape to the post. When the door is closed, its jamb will come in contact with the tape to form a mild seal.

If the roof structure is not included in painting plans, cover it with wide paper and tape. Spray painting creates a lot of overspray, some of which will land on the roof unless it is protected.

Tires and wheels must also be protected against overspray. Secure wide strips of paper to the fenderwells with tape. Make sure the paper is long enough to extend over the entire wheel and tire.

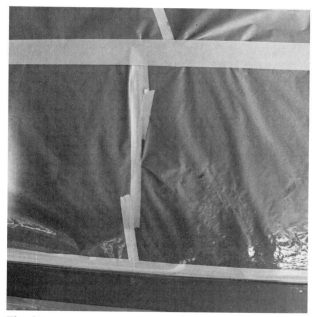

The shiny section at the bottom right corner shows where paint has been sprayed. If the seam between two sheets of masking paper had not been sealed with tape, air pressure from the paint gun could have forced the seam open to allow overspray to land on windows and trim underneath. Notice that 2 inch tape was used to secure the paper covering the windows to that covering the roof.

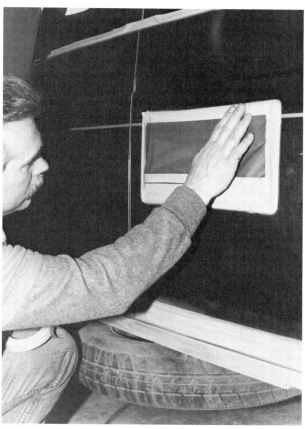

To cover the large recessed license plate area on Mycon's van, Laursen used a combination of masking paper and 2 inch tape. Any combination of paper or tape is fine, as long as it completely masks what it is intended to. Because they are generally hard to reach and difficult to work on, obstructed edges and recessed seams are the most prone to receiving overspray blotches. Take extra time along those items to be sure they are adequately masked.

Paint was sprayed on the hood and fender of this 4x4, as noted by the overspray on the paper covering the windshield. Paper was also placed over the uninvolved roof and rear section in order to protect them against overspray. Note that the wheel is covered with a disposable tire cover, available at autobody paint and supply stores.

8

Paint Application

The method you use to apply paint to your car's body depends upon how extensive the overall job is going to be. Small accents like monochromatic trim may be most easily blacked out with a can of quality spray paint. Small graphics requiring only a pint of paint can be handily sprayed with a maneuverable detail spray gun. Large jobs like panels and complete repaints require the use of a large conventional spray paint gun system or an HVLP.

The mechanics of spray painting are basically the same for all application methods. You must maintain even coverage by holding the nozzle away from the surface the same distance for all passes, keep the spray

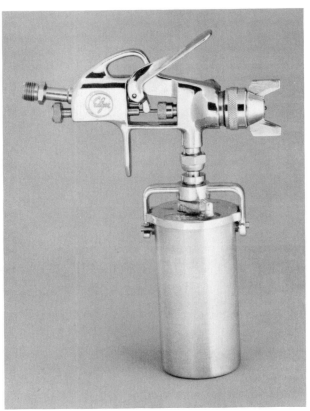

Touch-up spray paint guns, like this one from Eastwood, work great for applying slight accents and small graphics in tight areas and also for paintwork on small graphics or minimal design patterns. Custom painters frequently use this type of gun to apply second or third colors in a color-blend design. The Eastwood Company

Before the application of adhesion promoter or paint, Laursen roughs up the factory finish on Mycon's van with a Scotch-Brite scouring pad. The lighter color just ahead of his hand indicates the area has been scuffed already. Great pressure is not required, just enough to remove a finish's fine sheen.

84

Just before painting, surfaces should be wiped off with a tack cloth. An assortment of brands is available at autobody paint and supply stores. These tack clothes were displayed at Bel-Tech Auto Paint. Their purpose is to remove all remaining specks of sanding dust so that paint finishes turn out blemish-free.

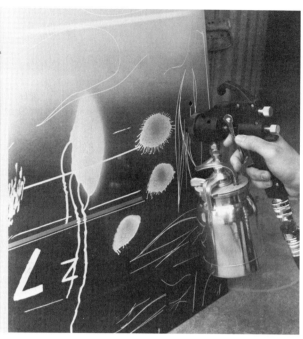

This test panel has been used for pinstripe, letter, spray painting and now freak drop practice. Novice custom painters are urged to practice with such panels in order to become familiar with painting equipment and application techniques. It is far better to get runs on a test panel, from holding a paint gun too close, than on the side of your favorite car.

The white paint on this Volkswagen Bug had to be cured before masking efforts could begin for the graphics. The design incorporates a green band around a blue box highlighted with green *streaks. Before second colors could be applied, flash times had to be honored to prevent sags, runs or wrinkles.* Steve Brown

tip perpendicular to the surface at all times and apply the same amount of paint with each pass.

Solid color lacquer-based paints are most forgiving. If a run or sag develops, you just have to wait ten to twenty minutes for it to dry and then sand it down with fine sandpaper. Enamels are less workable. Their application has to be done correctly the first time, which is the reason most experienced auto painters suggest novices start out with lacquer products.

Timing is a critical factor between coats. If a second or third coat is applied too soon, sags, wrinkles or other blemish problems will occur. It is imperative that you wait the prescribed time before adding successive coats. These times are listed on information sheets available from autobody paint and supply stores for whatever paint system you employ.

Test panels

As with masking, you should spend some time practicing with your paint gun. An old hood or trunk lid will serve well as a base for practice efforts. Use it to see what happens when the gun is held too close or too far away and how well paint flows when it is maintained at about 8 to 12 inches from the surface. Practice holding your hand straight and not twisting your wrist halfway through a pass.

Two knobs are located on the top rear part of spray guns. These regulate the spray fan and volume of paint dispersed. You should set the air pressure according to the instructions on the information sheet for the paint you are using. Then adjust the fan until you get a spray pattern that fits the work; wide fans are for large panels and tight fans for smaller areas.

Next, adjust the volume control knob so that the amount of paint flows on in a consistent manner. Too much paint exiting the nozzle will cause sags and runs and too little will result in light coats and streaks. Make a number of passes on your test panel until the adjustments show that paint flows on in an even and complete pattern.

Another adjustment for most spray guns is located at the nozzle opening; it is referred to as an air cap. A quarter turn will change the spray fan from a vertical shape to a horizontal one. When painting exterior car

Murdock is pointing to the paint volume control knob on the back of this full-sized paint gun. Turning this knob adjusts the amount of paint that will flow through the gun upon activation of the trigger. The knob just above that one adjusts the width of the fan spray; the more it is closed, the tighter the fan will be to eventually form a circle. Practice with these controls on a test panel to become confident and proficient with their use.

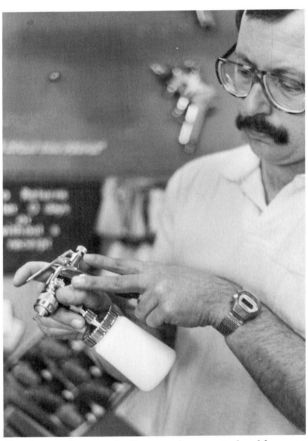

Touch-up paint guns also feature volume control and fan spray adjustment knobs, as Murdock indicates. Note the comfortable trigger assembly for this gun. It is activated by the full length of an index finger. For left-handed painters, most of these levers can be repositioned on the other side of the nozzle head.

bodies, horizontal passes are made and the fan should be set to fill a wide vertical pattern. This allows for as much paint coverage as possible with each pass. While painting in a vertical motion, like for doorjambs, the air cap can be set to give a horizontal fan. As necessary, adjust these fan directions and apply them to your test panel to see how well they work.

Painting with candy colors is difficult. The final depth of finish depends on how many coats were applied over the base coat. Working with a test panel will help you decide about how many coats will be needed to achieve the effect desired. Custom painters apply candy paint a little differently than regular products. In addition to making horizontal passes, they also make vertical ones. This is done in order to achieve thorough coverage and reduce the chances of streaking. Again, practice on a test panel to perfect this maneuver.

Pearls and metallics must be tested before actually being sprayed onto a car body. It is impossible to know just how much material will produce what effects unless you see it on a surface. Start out with just a minimal amount of pearl or metallic flakes mixed in with the paint and spray that on a test panel. If the results are satisfactory, fine. If not, you may need to add a little more in order to get the results desired.

Keep track of exactly how much pearl or metallic you put into quantities of paint. This way, once you reach just the right ratio you will be able to mix up new batches to the same consistency. Air pressure and the distance between the paint gun and surface will also affect the color of pearls, metallics and candies.

Paint and solvent mixing

Measuring sticks are available at autobody paint and supply stores. These items show you how much solvent thinner or reducer or hardener to add per a certain quantity of paint. Some paint mixtures, like candy lacquer, may have to be thinned 400 percent with solvent. This is so extra-light coats of paint can be applied to gradually develop darker colors. It may take

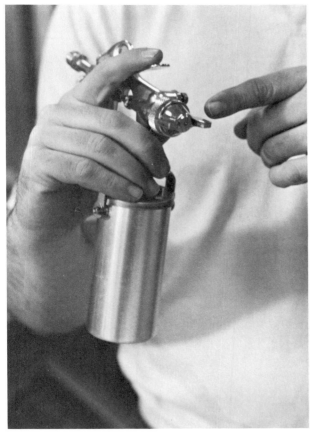

The air cap located at the tip of touch-up paint guns operates the same as for full-sized paint guns. In the position indicated here, the fan spray will be vertical. This is because air pressure forced out of the wing-like appendages (just below Murdock's finger) will blow against paint as it exits the gun, in a sense pushing it into a vertical pattern. If the wing adjustments were moved a quarter turn so that they were located on top and bottom, air pressure from them would cause the fan spray to come out in a horizontal pattern.

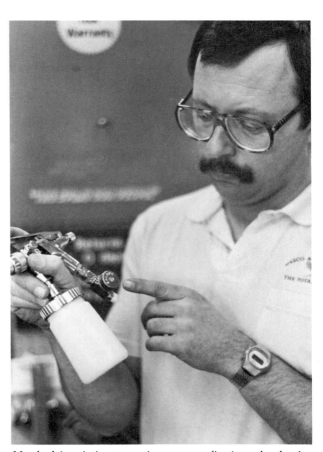

Murdock is pointing to an air-pressure adjusting valve that has been attached to a touch-up spray gun. After the air compressor pressure has been set to prescribed psi settings, this additional valve can be used to fine-tune air pressure for delicate paintwork. Adjusting the valve and testing the fan spray for pattern and paint application is best done on a test panel prior to use on a car finish.

up to thirty extra-light coats to develop just the right shade.

Mycon uses a clean, empty paint can for this mixing process because of its stable base and wide opening. That mix is then poured through a standard paint filter which rests at the top of his paint gun's cup. To ensure the paint in your gun's cup is pure, always strain mixtures through filters. Paper filters for this process are inexpensive and readily available at autobody paint and supply stores.

Mixing the correct amounts of paint, solvent or hardener is critical. Too much solvent may cause paint to run easily and too little may result in paint splatter or a clogged gun nozzle. The same is true with hardener; too much may cause cracking and too little might prevent paint from setting up or curing for hours, resulting in sags. After mixing all of the ingredients, be sure the caps are replaced on all the products. This will prevent accidental spills and also help to reduce evaporation of the products.

Murdock says that all of the jobbers he knows wear gloves while mixing paint. He expects they will soon be required to wear respirators as well. You should consider these same safety precautions when mixing paint, solvents and hardeners. You also must be keenly aware of any heat sources located within your work area. Vapors from almost all paint products are flammable and could be ignited by pilot lights or other open flames. Professional body shops keep fire extinguishers handy just in case they are needed, and you should too.

To keep paint from filling the little groove around the edge of a paint can's opening, use a small nail and a hammer to poke a few holes in the groove at one point along the edge, say five holes in an inch-wide space. These holes will allow paint to flow back into the can instead of laying around in the groove to make a mess when the lid is replaced. Lay a heavy rag over the entire lid to keep residual paint in the groove from splattering you when tapping the lid back in place.

Mixing candy concentrates, pearl and metallic flakes must be done according to the manufacturer's recommendations. These will be plainly listed on the information sheets provided by the autobody paint and supply store. Since metallic flakes or pearls cannot be taken out of a mixture if their content is too heavy, Mycon prefers to start out with a weaker mix and run a

Mycon and Laursen highly recommend that all metallic pearl and candy paint be sprayed onto a test panel before being sprayed on a car. This is the best way to actually see how the paint mix turned out and how its application is presented before *taking a chance on an inferior mixture blemishing an auto finish. This is also an excellent way to determine if spray paint guns are operating as expected. Dan Mycon*

How to use your mixing stick:

Two Step Mixing:

1. Place the stick in a straight, flat bottom container with the measurements facing you.
2. Pour the first ingredient up to (for example) #2 in the left hand column.
3. Pour the appropriate hardener or reducer/thinner to the same number in the second column.

   Now you have the correct mixture. If more product is needed, pour all ingredients to a higher number, i.e., pour to #3.

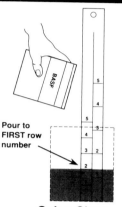

Pour to FIRST row number

Color, Clear or Undercoat

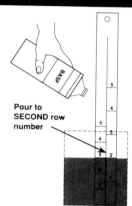

Pour to SECOND row number

Reducer/Thinner or Hardener

Three Step Mixing:

1. Place the stick in a straight, flat bottom container with the measurements facing you.
2. Pour the first ingredient up to (for example) #3 in the left hand column.
3. Pour the appropriate hardener to the same number in the second column.
4. Pour the appropriate reducer/thinner to the same number in the left hand column.

   Now you have the correct mixture. If more product is needed, pour to a higher number, i.e., pour to #4.

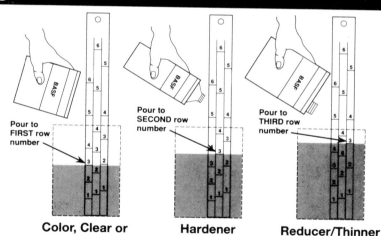

Pour to FIRST row number

Color, Clear or Undercoat

Pour to SECOND row number

Hardener

Pour to THIRD row number

Reducer/Thinner

Things to Do:

- Place stick into mixing container straight.
- Use a container with a flat bottom.
- Use a container with straight sides.
- Use the stick with the correct ratio for that product.
- Mix only what you need.
- Start at the left row and work right.
- Use the same number in each column.

Things Not to Do:

- Do not use a container with angled sides.
- Do not skip columns.
- Do not use a stick that has a ratio that is different than what the product calls for.

Auto paint is only as good as its mix and application. Mixing sticks are designed to make paint and solvent mixing easy and hassle-free. Directions are easy to follow, as indicated here with a sample of instructions for BASF two-step and three-step mixing sticks. Not all sticks are calibrated the same. You must use a mixing stick designed for use with the paint system you are mixing. BASF Corporation

This is the paint mixing area inside the enclosed, fireproof paint room at Newlook Autobody. You can tell that a lot of paint has been mixed here over the years. In the background is a paint code microfiche for determining specific paint color concentrate ratios and a scale used to measure mixtures. Using a clean empty can, Mycon is mixing Sikkens reducer with a custom Sikkens color according to a Sikkens paint stick calibration. Inserted into the paint gun cup just behind the can of Sikkens paint is a paint filter.

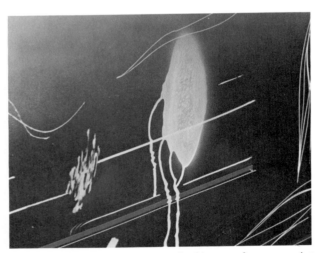

Runs like this should never occur. In this case, the spray paint gun was held too close to the surface. The same kind of problem could occur if inappropriate solvent-to-paint mixtures were made. A variety of other paint problems will also occur if too much or too little solvent or catalyst is added. Be sure to read and follow all paint-mixing instructions before mixing anything.

few passes over a test panel. If the mix is too weak, he simply adds more.

Paint gun techniques

Paint gun maneuvers do not make custom paint designs. Special effects are not created by thrashing paint guns around in wild circular patterns, upside down motions or any other such unconventional movement. Designs are a blend of masking endeavors, color options, paint additives and color blending. In almost every case, paint guns are employed in exactly the same fashion—smooth, even and controlled passes. Before painting, adjust the air pressure regulator to the psi setting recommended by the paint application guide while the spray gun is flowing air at full volume. This will guarantee that the proper pressure will exit through

Almost all auto paint products are flammable. In certain cases, a spark or open flame located a long way from your operation could cause vapors to ignite. Along with eliminating all pilot lights and smoking materials in the workplace, have a quality fire extinguisher with a minimum rating of 2A:10BC on hand.

the gun with the correct pressure at the tip while paint is sprayed.

Spray patterns

Even though practice on a test panel will give you experience with fan and volume controls, there are times during a paint process when you might want to check or change the fan or volume. If the job you are doing features a lot of masking paper over windows, you can run a test pattern on it. If not, have a long sheet of masking paper or a test panel handy for adjusting and testing these control items before applying them to the car.

Solid paint colors without additives are sprayed on cars in a horizontal line. Starting from one end of the car, you begin painting and do not stop until you reach the other end. In the case of masked sections, you paint from one end to the other in a continuous motion. Never stop midway between a pass. This will cause paint build-up, runs, sags or a host of other problems.

To prevent paint build-up on the edges of paint surfaces, keep moving the paint gun past the edge of the section; don't just stop at the end. Mycon starts air

This is a pneumatic paint can shaker at Newlook Autobody. Mycon uses it to thoroughly mix paint. This is an especially important thing to remember when mixing metallics or pearls. You can have the autobody paint and supply jobber mix your paint for you when you buy it, but remember to stir in metallic or pearl ingredients to maximum efforts as indicated by instructions.

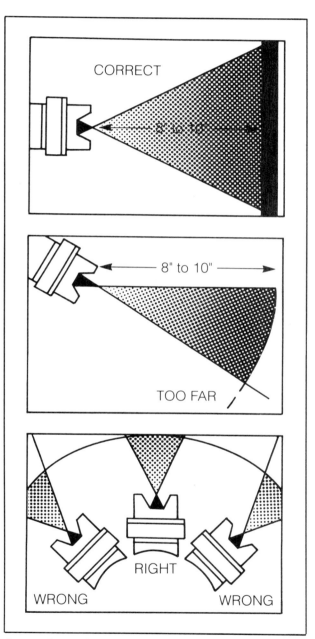

Spray paint nozzles must remain perpendicular with the surface upon which they are spraying. Deviations from this pattern will result in paint sags, build-up, orange peel and a host of other problems. Practice on a test panel will help you to lock your wrist and elbow, making your body move so that the spray gun remains in the same plane while spraying. PPG Industries

91

flowing through his gun away from the edge and then gently pulls the trigger until paint is flowing by the time the nozzle reaches the surface to be painted. At the other end, he continues painting and does not release the trigger until the gun has passed the last edge. In one long, even stroke, paint is deployed just before the gun reaches the first edge and is not stopped until it is past the last edge. This ensures that an equal amount of paint is sprayed on every part of the body during each pass of the spray gun.

You must not arc the pass at the end of a panel or masked area. The gun has to be maintained in a perpendicular position throughout the entire pass. If you were to flick your wrist at the end of a pass just to catch the last section of a panel, the amount of paint applied to that section will be less than that applied to the rest of it. Wrist movement during a paint pass should be avoided. To ensure this, lock your wrist and forearm in a solid position. Make your body move so that the paint gun stays exactly in one plane while the paint is sprayed.

Passes and coats

Painting starts at the top and works down. Since you will want each pass to overlap by half, start the first one with half of its vertical fan spray going onto masking above the job and the bottom half of its spray onto the work surface. The second pass will be a bit lower, and its full fan will reach from the bottom of the masking material to its own full vertical width below. The next pass will have the top half of its fan over the bottom half of the preceding fan and its bottom half covering an unpainted surface. In other words, only the bottom half of each fan spray will touch an unpainted surface. The top half of each fan will go over paint just applied during the previous pass.

There are times during painting that you may want to check the fan spray. Mycon did this while applying the white base coat to his wife's van, as noted by the two paint lines on the masking paper located in the middle of the center window area. If possible, have a test panel or at least a long sheet of masking paper available during your spray paint activities to allow you an opportunity to test fan sprays as needed.

CANDY APPLE Color Fast Transparent Acrylic Lacquer

1. Mix thoroughly and strain. Reduce 1 part Candy Apple to 1½ parts Metalflake Thinner.
2. Prepare surface:
   A. If surface is stripped bare, sand with oscillating sander using #180 grit paper. Wash thoroughly with a metal conditioner.
   B. If the existing surface is a factory baked finish in good condition, scuff with #400 sand paper and apply a bleeder-sealer before applying a ground coat. Otherwise, we recommend removing finish down to original surface. (A bleeder-sealer should be used over all Metalflake primers and other existing finishes.)
3. Prime with 3 coats of Metalflake Primer-Surfacer. Allow 15 minutes drying time between first two coats and 45 minutes after final coat. Sand with #360 grit paper.
4. Apply 3 coats of either Metalflake White Acrylic Lacquer, Gold Groundcoat, Silver Groundcoat, Ultrabrilliant Silver Groundcoat, Ultrabrilliant Gold Groundcoat, or Micro-Glow Silver or Gold. Allow 15 minutes drying time between coats.
5. Apply 3 or 4 coats of Metalflake Candy Apple, alternating spraying direction with each coat. Exception: Apply 6 to 8 coats of C-25 Candy Apple Red.

Alternate spray pattern with each coat to avoid streaking.

SPRAY PATTERN:

First Coat

Second Coat

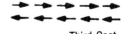

Third Coat

This is an illustration showing the instructions for applying Metalflake Brand Candy Apple Color Fast Transparent Acrylic Lacquer. Notice that it includes flash times. Also note the type of spray paint pattern suggested for their paint's application: first coat horizontal, second coat vertical, third coat horizontal and so forth. Metalflake Inc.

RECOMMENDED SPRAYING SEQUENCE

Cross-draft

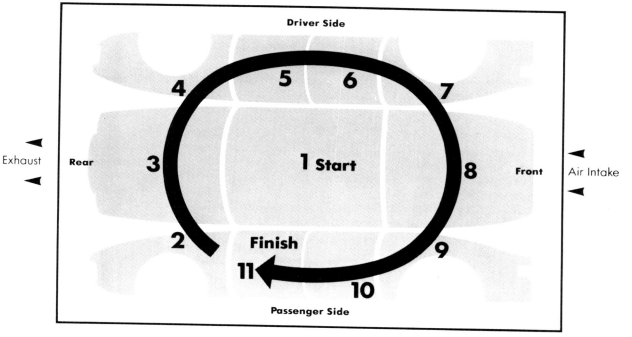

Down-draft

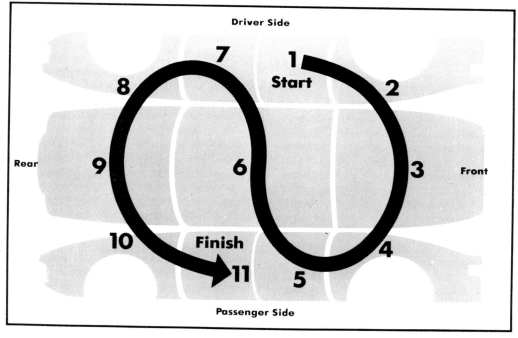

DuPont Company's recommended spraying sequence for full-body paint jobs. The illustration on top is for crossdraft paint booths and the one on the bottom for downdraft booths. Varia-tions of these patterns may be recommended by other paint manufacturers, and it is suggested you follow the pattern designated for the paint you are using. The DuPont Company

This process of covering each preceding pass with half of the new one is standard. It does not matter if you are painting an entire car or just a small section of one. These passes are not considered second coats either. That is simply the way a coat of paint is applied to a car body.

In some cases second coats are applied just a bit differently, depending upon the type of paint mixture you are using. Solid colors get exactly the same treatment for second and third coats as just described: horizontal applications with each pass overlapping the previous one by half a fan spray.

Candies, pearls and metallics are different. Their second coats are applied vertically, meaning the paint gun is passed from top to bottom and bottom to top, each overlapping the previous one by half a fan spray. Third coats are applied horizontally, just like the first. The reason this is done is to keep successive candy coats from streaking, and to make sure pearl and metallic flakes are applied as evenly as possible.

For complete paint jobs, there are specific patterns manufacturers recommend for paint application. Never start or stop painting in the middle of a panel. For

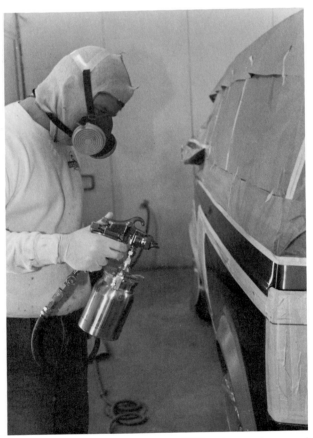

Mycon is holding the Accuspray HVLP paint gun in a good position just prior to applying a white base coat to his wife's van. His wrist and elbow are locked in position and he is ready to apply paint from right to left. Note the cap, respirator, long-sleeve sweatshirt and rubber gloves he is wearing.

example, do not start in the middle of the right fender and then walk around the front to finally end up in the middle of the fender. Paint an entire panel at one time, not half now and half later. Some patterns suggest starting at the roof and then working toward the hood, a front fender, then door, quarter panel, trunk, the other side and finally ending up at the hood again.

The pattern you choose is up to you, but be sure you have a plan in mind before you start. Consider where the hose will be while painting a certain area and how far the hose will reach. You will want the entire painting process to go smoothly, as if it was done in one fluid motion.

This is also true with custom paint projects where just certain panels are painted. If graphics are planned for the front, hood, fenders and parts of both front doors, don't start painting in the middle of the hood. By the time you get back to it, the paint will have dried a little and inconsistencies in color may occur. In that case, start at a door and work your way around to the other door. This way the entire door, hood and front end panels will be painted as units.

Paint-gun-to-surface distance

The distance you hold a paint gun from the surface being painted is an important factor. Holding it too close will cause runs. Keeping it too far away will cause the paint to dry somewhat before it reaches the surface, resulting in orange peel or uneven cover patterns. This again is where a test panel will help you get the feel for the spray gun you use. A distance of between 8 and 12 inches is good for the application of spray paint, and you should practice maintaining this distance throughout your painting endeavor.

There are circumstances when you might want to create a custom design by holding a spray gun close to the surface. The formation of freak drops is commonly done with thinned paint applied close to a surface. While the center of the drop is relatively even, outer edges receive a blast of paint and air to create little fingers that extend outward. You will not be able to perfect this feature without practice. Most are effected using an airbrush, but many custom painters have had good luck making larger freak drops with detail guns and some full-size units.

With freak drops, the fan has to be turned down so that the spray pattern is as close to a circle as possible. As paint is applied, the trigger is released slightly so that only air is forced out of the gun. Air pressure causes paint to run away from the center of the drop to form fingers that reach out in various shapes. Practice on a test panel is required before attempting this design. Not only will you have to determine appropriate gun adjustments, paint will have to be thinned to a working mixture. You will also have to determine the amount of paint and air pressure required to develop drops of the size and consistency desired.

Operation of a spray paint gun is not really a high-tech process. You just have to remember the basics and think about what you are doing as you apply paint. Key factors include maintaining an equal dis-

Correcting distorted spraying patterns

When the gun is adjusted properly and held at the right distance from the painting surface, the pattern should resemble Figure 9. As you can see, it's an elongated ellipse with a uniform distribution of material over the entire area.

A split spray (Figure 10) or one that is heavy on each end of a fan pattern and weak in the middle is usually caused by atomizing air pressure too high for the viscosity of the paint material. Reduce the air pressure, then check that the fluid adjustment is open fully. Do not lower air pressure below the recommended pressure of the product being sprayed.

Where the air pressure is correct, a split pattern may be caused by attempting to get too wide a spray with thin material. To correct, open material control "B" (Figure 7) by turning counter clockwise, then turn spray width adjustment "A" clockwise (Figure 7). This reduces the width of the spray but will correct split spray.

Dry material in a wind port "M" (Figure 8) restricts air passage through it and produces a crescent shaped pattern like Figure 11. To correct this, dissolve

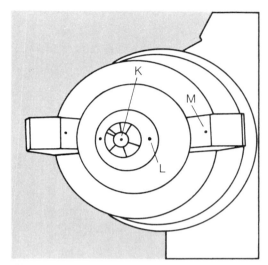

Figure 8.

material in the wing port with thinner, and clean out the port, but do not use metal instruments.

A spray pattern heavy and wider, at either top or bottom (see Figure 12), indicates that material has dried around the outside of the fluid tip.

Figure 9.

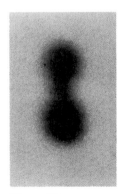

Figure 10.

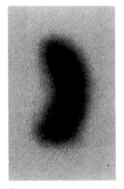

Figure 11.

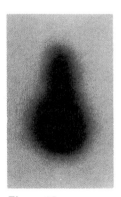

Figure 12.

Here are a series of inadequate fan sprays and the reasons why they have been affected. Dirty wind ports and other paint gun surfaces must be cleaned using quality solvent and only those brushes designed for paint gun cleaning. The use of hard-metal instruments can quickly and permanently damage paint gun components. PPG Industries

tance away from the surface at all times, long smooth passes and controlled application, so that the entire surface receives the same amount of paint with the same spray pattern.

Should you find that you are having trouble with paint blemishes and inconsistent coverage, stop painting and determine what is wrong. Doublecheck the paint mixture, use a test pattern to make sure the gun is operating properly and be sure your environment is dust free.

Maintenance and cleaning

A paint gun's physical condition is of equal importance to its fan pattern, volume control and air pressure.

Dirty tips or sticky valve stems will cause paint to splatter or fans to spray in unusual patterns. Many paint equipment suppliers, like Eastwood, sell spray gun cleaning brushes for a nominal price. Follow cleaning instructions supplied with your gun and use only those items which are specifically made for gun cleaning. Using wire or other hard items to clean out orifices and passageways will ruin a spray gun. All of the jets and openings are machined to exact standards for optimum operation. Scratches or chips along their edges will definitely affect spray patterns.

Spray paint guns must be cleaned after each use. Failure to do so will result in cured paint clogging fluid or air passageways. Once that happens, your gun is ruined and you'll have to buy a new one.

After each use, fill the paint cup a quarter full with an appropriate solvent. Swish it around to remove excess paint, primer or primer-surfacer. Fill the cup

Mycon has just completed a spray paint operation; note the painter's stocking cap on his head and respirator around his neck. The first thing he does after leaving the paint booth is clean his paint gun. Here, he uses lacquer thinner and a brush in a professional paint gun safety cleaning tub. Because he has taken meticulous care of his paint guns, they have lasted for years and still look brand new. Notice Mycon is wearing rubber gloves, the same ones he wore while painting.

After spending some time cleaning the paint gun from this Accuspray HVLP paint system from Eastwood, Steve Brown attends to a few drying details with a clean soft cloth. Inadequately cleaned painting equipment will fail in short time due to clogged jets and passageways. Meticulous care must be given spray paint guns if they are expected to last for any real length of time. As paint gun parts wear, kits can be purchased for most brands which will include all the parts needed to make them spray like new again. Tools courtesy of The Eastwood Company

Although Dan Mycon had a good idea of the graphic style he wanted to apply to his van, he made a simple tracing of the vehicle and sketched in his version. The paint color chips are from the Sikkens line. The color pen marks at the top were colors he was contemplating and the numbers written near them are paint codes. Bel-Tech Auto Paint of Bellevue, Washington, supplied paint for this project.

The ¾ inch masking tape is used to show how the graphic will look. Not only did this give Mycon a better idea of what the graphic would look like, it gave guidelines as to how far body filler and sanding efforts could extend to smooth out any nicks or dents in the body. The large area just above the lowest tape line will remain untouched, except for clear paint; Mycon did not want to have to touch up any areas in that section because of sanding marks.

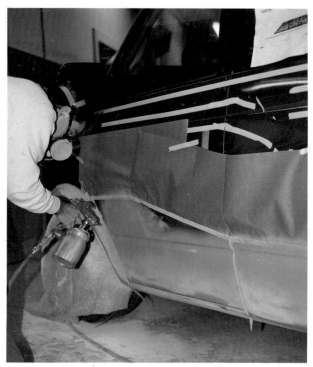

Mycon sprays on primer-surfacer to the entire area subjected to welding, grinding, body filler and sanding operations. This high-solid material will flow on easily to fill in any remaining imperfections. Notice that he is wearing a respirator during the procedure. Masking efforts at this point are still preliminary. Bodywork must be completed first before serious graphic masking can take place.

About two hours were spent perfecting just the right arc and point for the design. Just as one part would take shape, the other would appear too narrow, wide or uneven. The arc had to be symmetrical, too. This extra time paid off, as the graphic turned out great. Paint will be applied to the bottom of this Fine Line tape. Therefore, the point has to be trimmed to perfection. Mycon uses a sharp razor blade to carefully trim tape. Dull blades would only cause tape to wrinkle and possibly pull away from the surface. A gentle touch is required for this kind of trimming, as too much pressure will cut into paint. It is much better to make two or three light passes with the blade than a single heavy one.

A Sikkens urethane paint system will be used to apply the graphics to this van. R-M Cleaner, a compatible wax and grease remover, was used to remove all traces of wax, silicone or dirty residue. The factory paint finish was then scuffed with a Scotch-Brite pad after wax and grease remover cleaning. In the paint booth, you can see that the van is masked and just about ready for paint. A couple of chores still remain, though, like masking the roof and the application of an adhesion promoter. Note that masking tape alone was used to cover the taillight and a short section of the thin graphic extending from the rear toward the front in the middle of the body.

Mycon applied a white base coat using the Accuspray high-volume, low-pressure paint system, courtesy of The Eastwood Company. The white base coat is required for the three-step Sikkens paint system and color combination chosen for this project. After the base coat had dried according to the manufacturer's specifications, this purple color coat was sprayed on. The exposed white base coat above the purple is a combination of the masked charcoal area and another area that will be painted a different color. Mycon's expert paint application prevented purple from covering the base coat section where the next color will be sprayed.

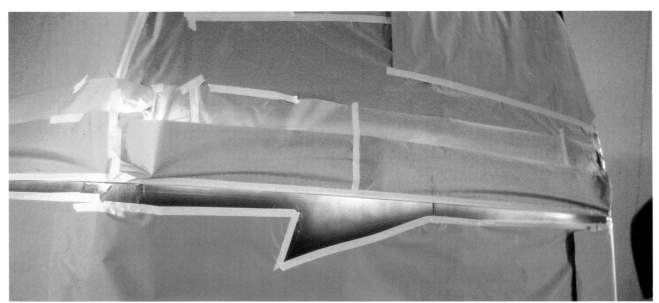

The lower sheet of wide masking paper covers the purple already sprayed. This masking effort did not have to be perfect as it is simply attached to the already masked charcoal section. A new color will be sprayed along this graphic strip, and the Fine Line tape used to mask off the charcoal section will also serve as the bottom border for the section.

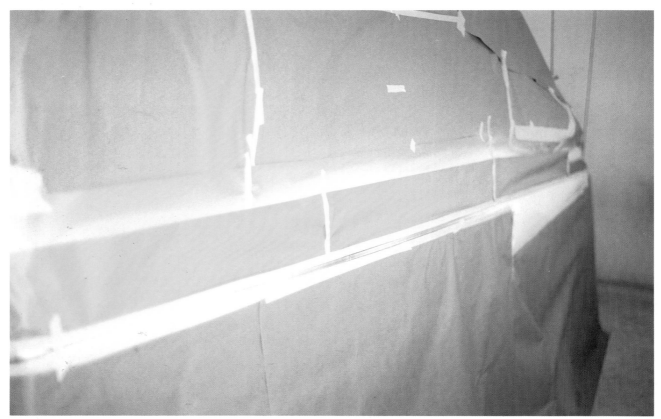

With all this masking paper, it is hard to see just what is supposed to be painted. This effort will allow painting of a thin line that extends from the back of the van to form an arc and point on the front door. New masking was also added just above the line to be painted, as noted by the white base coat overspray located just above it. Continued masking during a professional paint operation requires a quick-drying paint; otherwise, painters could have to wait for days before applying new graphics. Lacquer-based paints' quick-drying nature comes in handy for professionals and for you at home.

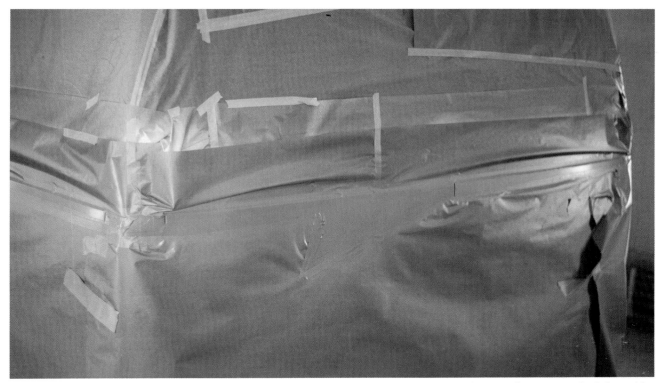

This shows the outline of blue paint applied to the graphic. Note the amount of overspray applied to the masking paper. This is normal and in fact planned. Overlapping fan sprays are used to apply paint so that each section of the body receives exactly the same amount of paint. There is still one more color left to add to this design. When the blue is dry, it will be masked off and another section unmasked for paint application.

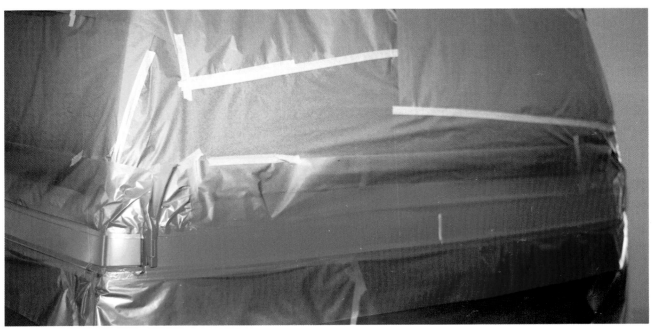

A reddish-pink paint has been sprayed on the top graphic line section. Notice that color coats were applied from bottom to top; once a bottom section is covered and masked, it is protected from any paint runs. The section of masking paper just below the reddish-pink color covers the freshly applied blue paint. The short line of masking tape located in the middle of the reddish-pink paint at the center of the doors is an exposed piece of masking tape used to seal the gap between doors. A section of tape that covered this tape was, of course, painted red but pulled off before this photo was taken.

With some masking paper removed, you can see the graphics pattern and color combination. The arc and point design on this door is the one Mycon and Bruce Caldwell spent two hours applying. Getting both arcs and points exactly the same was not easy, not even for the professional. Designing and masking efforts take time to implement, but the results can be fantastic.

In the sunshine, this graphics design looks pretty good. The color combination is appealing, and the pattern is subtle yet striking. Clear paint has been applied and the van is ready for wet sanding and buffing. The bumpers have been painted but will not be installed until this paint has been completely sanded and compounded.

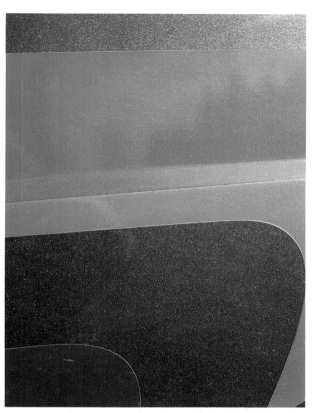

As orange peel or nibs are found, Mycon wet sands; the white residue is a sign that clear paint is being wet sanded. As he continues along the body, Mycon looks at the finish from ground level. He figures that if the finish looks good from that angle, it will look good from an upright position. Notice that masking paper is still in place. This is so that buffing compound will not splatter all over the clean paint and, in case more clear paint is needed, major masking will not have to be duplicated. Mycon is using a 1450 rpm buffer and a soft sponge-like pad to polish the new paint.

This close-up photograph clearly shows the metalflakes in the charcoal color and pearl sparkles in the other colors. Sharp paint edges are magnified by a build-up of compound. This residue is quickly removed by cleaning the surface with wax and grease remover. Dunn will pinstripe these edges to flatten and perfect them.

The purple bumpers match the lower graphic section on Mycon's van. The plastic adhesion promoter worked well, as paint evenly covers the bumpers' vinyl attributes. Care must be given during the installation of the bumpers on the van so that they are not scratched or chipped.

Mycon's van sports its new graphics well. The paint has been wet sanded and compounded with all nibs removed. Masking paper has been cleared off and bumpers installed. Finishing touches will include subtle pinstripes to outline each graphic line, paint-ing of the A-pillar black to match the rest of the window area circumference and painting of the fenderwells black to make them look crisp.

again, about a quarter full, and attach it to the gun. Spray all of the fresh solvent out of the gun, preferably toward an open area and not at the car. Put a rag over the nozzle and put your finger over it to plug the opening. Pull the trigger and allow air pressure to backwash the siphon unit. Swish the mixture by shaking the gun and expel all remaining solvent. Kosmoski conveys his tenacity for equipment maintenance by telling his painters that he never wants to know what color was sprayed through the paint gun the last time. This means that each and every drop of paint must be thoroughly removed from all parts of the assembly.

Take the air cap off of the gun and clean it with an appropriate brush. Be sure to use clean solvent and make certain all traces of paint are removed. Use rags to thoroughly clean the cup and top of the gun assembly. Brushes make quick work of removing paint splatter from exterior surfaces. Dry the inner passageways by flowing air through the unit and the exterior parts by using a clean cloth.

Never lay a gun assembly on its side. Paint could flow back into the passageways to dry and clog them.

Always hang the unit upright. A simple hanger can be made by fastening a small piece of dowel under a shelf or attaching a length of heavy wire under a workbench overhang.

Air and fluid valve stems are short rods that run from the gun handle to the trigger or from the nozzle assembly to the trigger. Attached to them is a small retainer nut. Sometimes these valves get sticky and will adversely affect spray patterns. According to maintenance directions supplied by the manufacturer, loosen retainer nuts and apply a few drops of machine oil to the rods. This will lubricate the mechanisms and allow for free and easy movement with no sticking or spray pattern disfigurements.

Color blending

Putting on a set of flames or graphics utilizing more than one color in a blended design requires a slightly varied form of spray gun control. Basically, instead of ensuring that equal paint coverage is maintained throughout the process, painting is stopped at a point where color blending is desired.

The yellow flames on this 1958 Chevrolet are accented with red toward the end of flame lick tips. After the yellow base color had dried according to the paint's instructions, red was gradually added. Some painters prefer to start with the darkest end first and gradually release the paint gun trigger to fade out the color.

Others fade it in lightly and gradually increase flow for maximum coverage. Once again, novice custom painters must practice color blending on a test panel to perfect this technique. Dan Mycon

This street rod panel delivery sports an exquisite orange paint job featuring pink front fenders and running boards with a hint of pink touching the rear fenderwell lips and flaring out at the rear bumper. The scallops are pink with a brighter orange accent. Custom color coordination and masking techniques make this vehicle stand out crisp and pristine. Dan Mycon

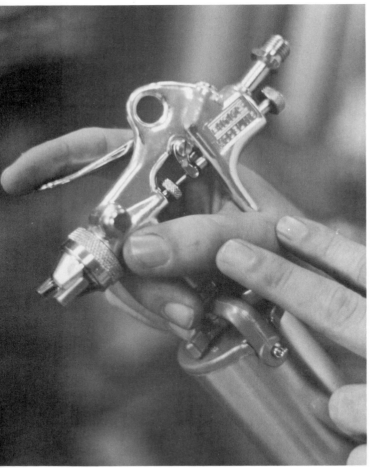

This is the proper way to hold a touch-up spray gun. Your index finger will control the flow of paint while your thumb and remaining fingers secure the gun in your hand. Your free hand should be holding the air hose to be certain it is not dragged across the car.

For instance, say you want to blend orange and then red to a base of yellow flames. You will not have a definite masking point from which to begin, as the colors will just blend at some point. Therefore, you start painting the second color at the point where it will be most solid. As you move toward the area where the second color will be blended, you simply start to release the trigger and gradually restrict paint flow until it completely stops. Stopping abruptly will cause a distinct blend edge as opposed to a gradual blend.

Custom painters have their special ways of blending colors together on a surface. Some prefer to start with darker color bases first and then blend in lighter ones. Others start with the lights and then work in the dark. You will have to practice with a test panel to see which method works best for your design motif.

It is important to note that lower pressures will result in the least amount of overspray. Use a test panel to determine the lowest pressure setting you can work with and still get an adequate and smooth blending coverage.

Detail paint guns generally work best for making flames and other color blending. Their small size makes them maneuverable, and since a small amount of paint is all that is required, their capacity is ideal.

Overspray sanding may be required in some cases in order to get blend designs to look their best. The type of paint you use for this blending endeavor is therefore important. Lacquers work well because they dry fast and can be worked on in just twenty to thirty minutes after being sprayed. Color sanding at this point is critical. Use very-fine-grit sandpaper, like 1000 to 1500. Too much sanding may leave the design looking awkward and touch-up hard to accomplish. Go slow and thoroughly contemplate your moves before you make them.

By adding color concentrate a little at a time, you can create a color scheme where shades darken as paint approaches the lower sections of a vehicle. First, spray the upper portion with a color mixture that suits your eye. Then add a few drops of color concentrate and spray that just below your first two to three passes. Follow that with a few more drops of concentrate and a couple of more lower passes. Follow this pattern until you reach the bottom of the car. By feathering in each spray fan, a gradual color change will be featured showing the lightest color at the top and darkest at the bottom.

Flash times

Enough time must be allotted between coats of paint to let solvents evaporate. These times are referred to as flash times. In the Metalflake Product Application Guide for their Universal Candy Concentrate, it is recommended you wait at least fifteen minutes between coats. This is so solvent from the first coat can evaporate and will not become trapped by subsequent coats.

Different paint coatings require various flash times. For instance, recommended flash times for

PRODUCT APPLICATION GUIDE SUPPLEMENT
UNIVERSAL CANDY CONCENTRATE

1. Suggested Mixing Ratio:
   A. Mix 4 ounces of Candy Concentrate to 1 quart of Clear, or 1 pint to 1 gallon of Clear. Follow the Clear manufacturer's thinning recommendations, application procedures, and drying times. If using a ready-to-spray urethane Clear, reduce the mixing ratio of Concentrate to Clear to allow for applying the same number of coats as used with a reducible Clear to obtain the desired color.

2. Prepare Surface:
   A. If surface is stripped bare, sand with oscillating sander using #180 grit paper. Wash thoroughly with a metal conditioner.
   B. If the existing finish is a factory baked finish in good condition, scuff with #400 grit sandpaper and apply a bleed-sealer before applying a ground coat. Otherwise, we recommend removing the finish to bare metal. (A bleeder-sealer should be used over all primers and other existing finishes.)

3. Prime with 3 coats of Metalflake Primer-Surfacer. Allow 15 minutes drying time between first two coats and 45 minutes after final coat. Sand with #360 grit sandpaper.

4. Apply 3 coats of your choice of Metalflake's groundcoats. Allow 15 minutes drying time between coats.

5. Apply 3 or 4 coats of Concentrate/Clear mix, alternating spraying direction with each coat. Because of the highly transparent pigmentation used in our Candy Concentrates, care must be taken to insure that uniform coats are applied to avoid light and dark shadings. Colors deepen as more coats are applied. Allow 15 minutes drying time between coats.

6. Final Finishing:
   A. Topcoat with 3 or more coats of the same Clear vehicle as used for the Concentrate/Clear mix and follow the manufacturer's application procedures and drying times.

PRODUCT APPLICATION GUIDE SUPPLEMENT
FLIP-FLOP AND STAR-PEARL CONCENTRATES (LEAD)
AND DRY POWDERS (NON-LEAD)

1. Suggest Mixing Ratio:
   A. Mix 1 ounce or more of the Concentrate or Powder color to 1 quart of ready-to-spray Clear. Follow the Clear manufacturer's application procedures, and drying times.

2. Prepare Surface:
   A. If surface is stripped to metal, sand with oscillating sander using #180 grit sandpaper. Wash thoroughly with a metal conditioner.
   B. If the existing surface is a factory baked finish in good condition, scuff with #400 grit sandpaper and apply a bleeder-sealer before applying a groundcoat. Otherwise, we recommend removing the finish to bare metal. (A bleeder-sealer should be used over all primers and other existing finishes.)

3. Prime with 3 coats of Metalflake Primer-Surfacer. Allow 15 minutes drying time between first 2 coats and 45 minutes drying time after final coat. Sand with #360 grit sandpaper.

4. Apply 3 coats of Metalflake's White Acrylic Lacquer. Allow 15 minutes drying time between coats.

5. Apply 2 or more light coats of the Concentrate or Powder/Clear mix. Alternate spraying direction with each coat to avoid streaking.

6. Final Finishing:
   A. Topcoat with 3 or more coats of the same Clear vehicle as used for the Concentrate or Powder/Clear mix and follow the manufacturer's application procedures, and drying times.

This supplement sheet was included in a pamphlet which listed application guidelines for Metalflake automotive paint products. This guide shows how to mix and apply Metalflake's Universal Candy Concentrate, Flip-Flop and Star-Pearl con- centrates and dry powders. While making your auto paint purchase, be sure to retrieve application guides for all of the products you will be using. Metalflake Inc.

Metalflake CrystaCryl Clear or PolyGloss Clear are one hour between the first two coats and four hours between the second and third coats. It is also suggested you wait at least three days before wet sanding with 600 grit paper.

Every paint manufacturer has its own set of recommended flash times. This information is printed on information sheets and, in most cases, included on the labels of the products themselves.

Paint coats and thickness

The number of paint coats applied to a surface depends on the type of paint used and what is being covered. Candy colors may require three coats of base color, three to four coats of candy color and up to six coats of clear. Two- and three-step systems of other paint types can require the same. With this much paint on a car body, it is extremely important to recognize and adhere to suggested flash times. Failure to do so may result in weak, sagging or wrinkled paint.

Enamel paint generally covers in just two coats; depending upon the color being covered, it may take three. Since enamels cannot be repaired like lacquers, you have to be sure each coat is properly applied. Flash times for enamels are critical because they dry in two ways—by solvent evaporation and by oxidation. Application of additional coats too soon will result in runs.

Reading the instructions on information sheets and product labels is important. You can estimate drying times by feel and gloss, but you always risk the chance of painting too soon. In too many cases, like with enamels, candies, pearls and metallics, one mistake can ruin an entire paint job, requiring you to start over at the beginning after stripping blemished paint. For best results, follow instructions and paint according to the prescribed procedures.

9

Special Custom Paint Tricks and Traditions

Throughout the years, custom painters have developed their own unique style of customizing cars with various paint maneuvers. Cobwebbing was popular for a time, as were lace painting and murals. Times change and fads come and go. In the 1960s and 1970s, vans were popular and so were murals and psychedelic designs. The 1980s brought in a new wave of custom paint with wild graphics and subtle monochromatic effects.

Airbrush techniques

If you have ever attended a car show, chances are you have seen airbrush artists busily painting logos, cars and various character scenes on T-shirts. Airbrush work is unique since the airbrush can paint a thin line or be used to fog in wide paths to resemble anything from a desert floor to a skyline.

Airbrush units consist of a compressor, hose line and painting unit. They are available at artist supply stores and through mail order from Eastwood. They range in price from $160 for single-action models to around $200 for double-action units. The difference between a single- and double-action is that the double-action allows the user to control pattern width and paint flow with just one control. The single-action requires the nozzle tip be adjusted to change pattern width, an operation that cannot be done while in the middle of a stroke.

Custom auto painters use airbrushes in a number of different circumstances. They are quite commonly employed to accent graphics and lettering to make

This is a ¹/₁₀ horsepower airbrush compressor made by Paasche. Its extra-quiet operation is a real bonus while using it. This unit will supply adequate air pressure to both single- and dual-action airbrushes. Be sure to follow operational instructions. If the air line is not bled when the compressor is first started, the machine will pulsate to give an erratic air flow. Directions clearly explain the procedure. The Eastwood Company

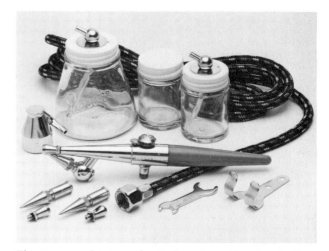

This is a complete Paasche single-action airbrush unit. Extra tips are provided which allow users to paint lines of various widths. An assortment of paint cups is provided for use during multiple color operations. Because of its fine spray paint features, airbrushes must be cleaned after each use; this is critically important when using lacquer-based paints. The Eastwood Company

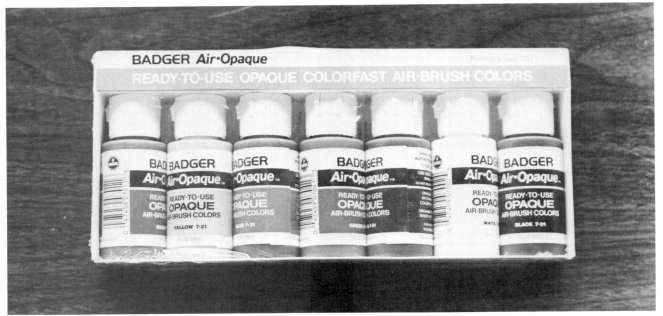

Ready-to-use airbrush paints are available at sign and artist supply stores. This collection is made available by Badger.

Various packages contain different color assortments and colors can be mixed to create new hues.

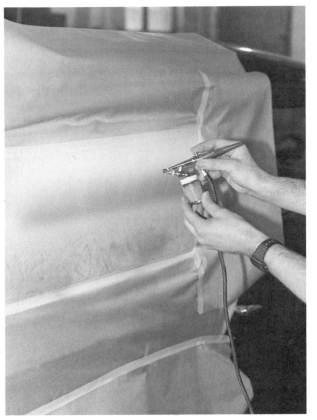

Dunn used this Paasche airbrush to paint the pink tint to the logo on his panel truck. Slow-drying enamel paint was mixed fifty-fifty with mineral spirits. To effect the blending at the top of the letters, he simply pulled the unit away from the surface to create an extra-wide fan that eventually dissipated.

them look three dimensional. On small jobs, painters use them exclusively instead of having to depend on a large air compressor and detail spray guns. As you learn how to control spray patterns, you will be able to work with stencils to design custom scenes, graphics and custom designs.

Airbrush work can produce a huge variety of custom paint schemes. Although the unit is too small to paint a car, it is used successfully for murals, landscape and seascape scenes, animated characters and detail work. Even though airbrush lines can be made sharp, most artists also employ delicate brushwork to outline and accent certain designs.

Operation

The most important thing to remember about airbrushes is that they can clog easily. Tiny air passages and paint tubes will quickly become blocked with dry paint if not cleaned immediately after use. You can use paint made just for airbrush work, lettering enamel or lacquer. Dunn always mixes lettering enamel fifty-fifty with mineral spirits when applying it through an airbrush. You should experiment with your airbrush to come up with a mixture and color tint that suits your needs and application.

Most painters use lacquer-based paints for custom airbrush design work. This is because lacquer dries quickly, allowing them to add additional coats soon after base coats have been sprayed. When spraying lacquer, you will have to be absolutely sure to clean the airbrush after each use, as lacquer's quick-drying nature can easily plug lines and spray tips if allowed to set up. This is also a concern when mixing lacquer and thinner. Normally, thinner is mixed with lacquer four-to-one and sometimes five-to-one to keep it from dry-

110

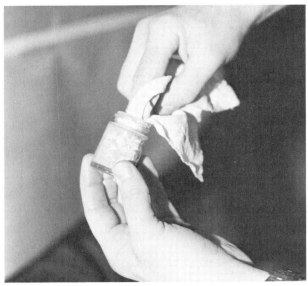

All parts of the airbrush system must be cleaned after use. This paint cup was rinsed with mineral spirits and is now being wiped out with a paper towel. Failure to properly clean the tool will eventually result in its failure. Paint flakes left in cups can pass through the system to clog tiny passageways.

The clean airbrush is allowed to operate in the wide-open position to blow out lingering mineral spirits or paint residue. Be careful with spray tips. They are fine machine parts that, if dropped, may well become dented or chipped which would render them nearly useless.

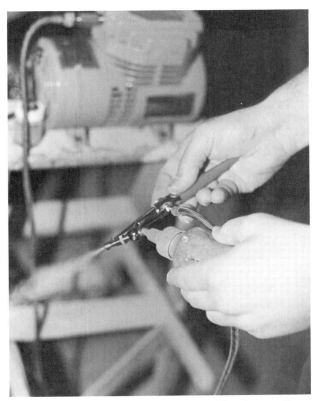

To quickly and thoroughly clean interior airbrush ports, Dunn lays the tip from the mineral spirits jug against the paint inlet opening. As the airbrush is operated, mineral spirits are poured in it to flush out all paint residue. To backflush the unit, mineral spirits are poured into a paint cup and the unit operated while a cloth is held over the nozzle.

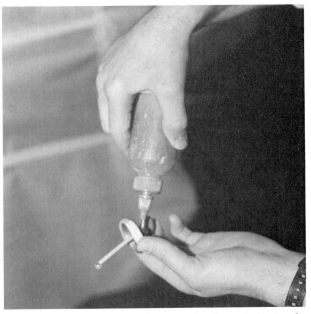

Flow tubes for paint cups also must be cleaned. Again, the handy spout on Dunn's mineral spirits jug comes in handy to flush out the tube on this cap. Air pressure from the airbrush can also be used to blow out remaining mineral spirits. Be sure to clean paint from around the cap threads.

ing too fast. Afterward, lacquer is always coated with clear to bring out a rich gloss.

Different tip sizes are available for airbrush nozzles. They are designated by numbers with the smaller numbers denoting smaller tips; that is, #1 is much smaller than #5. Small tips are used to paint fine lines, while larger tips are saved for jobs requiring wider patterns. Take good care of tips and needle valves. One small imperfection will ruin their spray pattern.

Clean airbrushes with the same solvent used to thin the paint used with them. After cleaning the paint reservoir, fill it a quarter full with solvent and spray it through the tool. Backflush the tool by holding a cloth over the nozzle and operating the trigger mechanism. Then, take the tip off and thoroughly clean the head assembly and needle valve.

Traditional custom effects

For special effects, you don't need much more than what is required for any other custom paint job. Generally, ultra-intricate designs are saved for panel inserts or other small spots. A detail paint gun is more appropriate for these efforts than a full-sized unit.

Lace painting

Lace painting is done by taping a piece of lace material over a finished base color and then painting over it with a different color. Fabric, which weaves the lace pattern together, prevents the new color from touching the base. The result looks like a sheet of lace has been embossed onto paint.

Cobwebbing

Cobwebbing is a process where thick paint is forced out of a gun at an unusually high pressure. Instead of flowing evenly and smoothly, paint comes out more like a thick goo to cover the surface in a series of stringy lines, like cobwebs or the lines found in marble.

This effect must be practiced before it is applied to a car body. You will have to determine which pressure setting works best along with how thick the paint must be to get the desired results. Most painters apply this technique while standing about three feet away from the surface to be covered. As the outcome dictates, they move closer or stand back farther. The closer it is applied, the more cobwebbing will group together. Conversely, as a gun is pulled farther away, cobwebbing is dispersed in a wider and more open design.

Because cobwebbing leaves a rather thick rough surface, clear coating is a must. It will take a number of coats to result in a smooth finish. Be sure the cobweb pattern is thoroughly dry before applying clear. Solvent bases in clear coats could dissolve parts of cobwebs to

This improvised heartbeat design did not require a lot of paint to complete. This kind of custom addition will take time to design, but actual painting could be done with a small touch-up gun and a minimal amount of paint. Special effects are generally saved for small areas, if for no other reason than to keep vehicles from becoming too overburdened or busy. Dan Mycon

make them lose their definition, flatten out and become less distinct.

Wrinkle finishes

To add a truly unique pattern to small body sections, painters have had good results applying plastic wrap or wrinkled aluminum foil over wet paint. Smearing plastic around creates an image that includes the base color as well as the top color in a swirl-like pattern. Wrinkled aluminum foil is just laid on top of wet paint to imprint designs. As the plastic or foil is removed from the surface, some wet paint comes with it to expose the underlying base.

To do this, the top paint must be wet. Professionals put retarder in paint instead of thinner (this project works best with lacquer) to keep it on the wet side. Note: the base has to be in good shape and already thoroughly cured.

Various effects have been made with sponges. Custom paint artist's use small sponges to dab paint on tree trunks in murals to make the tree look like it is full of leaves. All kinds of interesting designs can be made by dabbing different materials in paint and then gently dotting them onto a scheme.

Unique patterns are created when you lay down strips of masking tape in various configurations. Rectangles that intersect to create smaller boxes are popular. After the boxes have been made, certain ones are painted a different color than the rest to make the design stand out. This can be accomplished in a number of different ways.

You can lay tape patterns down on a good base and then paint over them. When tape is pulled, the original body color will show through. Or you can paint a panel one color, apply tape afterward and then blend other colors over the top. When the tape is pulled, a solid color will be confined into the space that the tape occupied.

Modern custom effects

In the 1990s, anything goes in custom painting from the subtle Euro-style monochromatic look to radical jagged-edged dry-brush painting and heartbeats.

Monochromatic styling

For the monochromatic look, or to black out aluminum or chrome trim, you will need a quality paint of

This custom sport truck is white with a set of three light-blue pinstripes located just above the lowest door panel section. Right above the pinstripes is an outlined scallop line filled in with pink splatter paint. A heartbeat design breaks up the splatter paint. This design is easily accomplished with One Shot Slow Drying Enamel Paint, some Finesse Pinstriping Stencil Tape and a couple of artist's paintbrushes. Steve Brown

A small graphic in gray and pink has been painted on the fan shroud of this custom Volkswagen Bug. Custom painting does not require a full-blown, all-out complete paint job. Simple additions like this help a vehicle to look different than others, therefore making it custom. In addition to the graphic, the distributor cap is pink and various engine parts are chrome, black and blue. Steve Brown

113

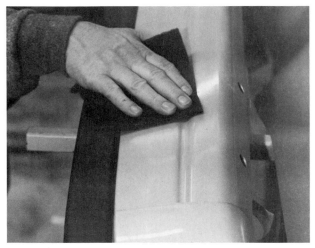

After bumpers have been cleaned and dried, their shiny painted surfaces are scuffed with a Scotch-Brite pad. This will give paint a better surface for bonding. Adhesion promoter should be used along with a flex additive for nonmetal parts. While scuffing, be sure all gloss has been cut down, as just one tiny spot left untouched could cause an eventual peeling problem.

the desired color and a scouring pad, like Scotch-Brite. Mycon simply roughs up the surface of such pieces with a Scotch-Brite pad to remove their shine and slick surface. This gives paint a finish to which it can adhere. After that, he puts on the color coat.

A custom painter could spend a lot of time preparing items like drip rail and window trim with coats of primer and sealer before painting. However, Mycon has found that one or two coats of paint alone seem to work just as well, as long as the pieces are properly scoured to a rough texture.

Masking trim pieces is critical. Just the slightest oversight will result in unwanted paint on a body surface or a missed spot on the trim item. In tight spots, use thin Fine Line tape to carefully mask along edges. Follow up with wider tape as the job demands. Be sure to cover large areas, like glass, with paper to prevent overspray problems.

Other accessories can be painted black or a color that matches the car body. Many enthusiasts include windshield wipers, radio antennas, door handles, key locks and light fixture trim in their custom design,

Individual pieces like bumpers, mirror housings and spoiler items should be painted separately, not while they are still on the vehicle. This is so that complete paint preparation efforts and coverage can be guaranteed. The use of sawhorses and wires may be needed to suspend pieces in accessible positions.

especially for the European monochromatic look. Accents, like subtle pinstripes, are added later.

Mycon had the grille of his 1988 Chevy sport truck powder coated black to finish off a monochromatic style. He did this in order to prevent expected rock chip damage from making this vulnerable piece look old and beat up. Street rodders have relied on powder coating for years to keep the frames on their cars from getting chipped by rocks and other road debris.

Plain steel wheels can be painted to match the car and fenderwells blacked out for a clean crisp appearance. Before putting your car back together, be sure you have completed all of the projects you had planned. This will save you the trouble of having to mask over sections again or removing parts that you just put back on.

Powder coating

Powder coating is an expensive process where a special colored powder is sprinkled onto an electrically charged metal part. After that, the part is put into an oven and baked. The result is a super-hard finish that resists rock chips and other road debris damage with outstanding durability.

Most home do-it-yourselfers will not have powder coating equipment and will have to hire out the work.

Dry-brush techniques

Before the 1980s, it seemed that custom painters and pinstripers recognized perfection by how crisp and clean paint lines were applied. Today, newer styles digress from crisp edges to include, of all things, paint-brush applications that look like they were brushed on. In fact, they are!

In their search to create new custom designs, paint artists have developed a design system called dry-brush. Roy Dunn uses this technique effectively to apply heartbeat designs that connect pinstripes. He has also applied dry-brush patterns to hoods, trunks, tailgates and other body sections to break up solid colors and add flair to overall jobs. As you walk through car shows, you will notice a lot of dry-brush applications done very tastefully.

Various brushes can be used for dry-brush designs. Dunn has had the best luck using small, stiff-bristle

The grille on Mycon's 1988 Chevrolet sport truck was powder coated in black. He had this done to finish off a monochromatic look and also to help the grille resist road debris and rock chip damage. Powder coating is an expensive procedure and colors are somewhat limited. A number of powder coating companies advertise in auto restoration and hobby magazines and are also listed in the telephone book yellow pages.

The leaf-spring shackle on this van was lightly covered with overspray. Since the rear bumper will completely cover it, overspray will not pose a problem. For other makes or models, this part may be clearly visible after the bumper is replaced. For those, you should consider painting the leaf-spring assembly with a quality black lacquer paint.

Ordinary steel wheels and certain parts of custom wheels can be painted the same color as your car or any other shade you desire. Here, a custom wheel is meticulously masked in preparation for custom paint. Wide tape is used to cover polished parts. Excess tape is trimmed off with a razor blade.

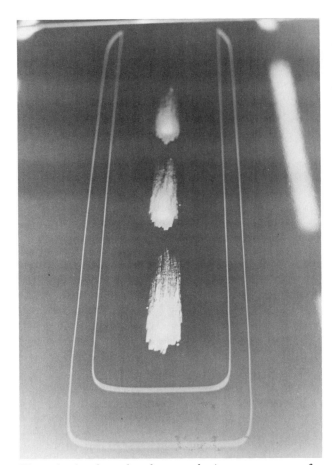

Three dry-brush strokes decorate the inner open area of a pinstripe hood design. More than one stroke was used to effect each of these marks. Some forethought was put into the plan, as the front parts are more solid while the tails trail off as if the brush ran out of paint. A wide variety of brush strokes, from these to really dry strokes, is the trick custom paint styles today.

Dry-brush designs are really nothing more than paint applied to the surface of a car with a paintbrush that is not completely wet with paint. Individual brush lines can be seen, and if it wasn't for the design, one would think a child had smeared a half-dried paintbrush across the finish of your car. Not too many years ago, people would have thought you were crazy to put a paintbrush to a car's finish.

For his brush-stroke work, Dunn prefers to use a small parts brush. The bristles are stiff to offer a unique application. Their cost is minimal, and he simply throws them away after each use. For the most part, the colors used for dry-brush painting are the same used for pinstriping. Therefore, paint is acquired from the same paper cup used to hold pinstripe paint.

parts brushes; they are inexpensive and readily available at auto parts and hardware stores.

Just a little paint goes a long way when effecting dry-brush techniques. You do not need a lot of paint on the brush. In fact, you need little, as the desired effect relies on skipped bristle strokes and a relatively open pattern.

To put on a heartbeat in an open section between a pinstripe, just dip one corner of the bristles in paint. Then carefully stroke the surface next to the front pinstripe with a fan-type motion. Start small and gradually increase the fan width to reach an apex point. After that, decrease strokes until you join with the pinstripe at the rear. Practice this technique a few times to become familiar with its ease of application and to realize how far to apply fan strokes.

Basic dry-brush strokes are just as easy to apply. For these, you should make sure that the full tip of the paintbrush is covered with a medium amount of paint. Application is made simply by brushing it on. If you don't like it, wipe it off with a paper towel and mineral spirits. Once a dry-brush design has been applied, you can dress it up by dotting a few orphan lines around it with just an edge of the brush.

Lettering

More and more, auto enthusiasts are making statements with their special vehicles by incorporating some sort of a written theme into their custom paint job. These range from small subtle names along pinstripe lines to large, bold letters that spell 4X4, Chevrolet, Ford and anything else one chooses.

Pinstripers have always had a knack for including their names somewhere in a pinstripe design. For that matter, expert pinstripers have even been known to draw stick figures of people in various positions that go completely unnoticed until one looks really close at the scene. Their creative talents can even go so far as to make a series of letters spell one thing from a distance, and something completely different when viewed from just inches away.

Painting letters on a car body requires a completely different set of brushes than pinstripes. Along with artist and sign supply stores, The Eastwood Com-

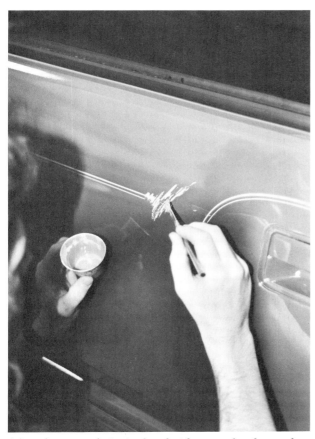

A heartbeat-type design is placed with a parts brush to make a dry-brush design that will connect the top pinstripes. Dunn takes his time and tries to paint each stroke so that it is balanced with the others. Held at a sharp angle to the surface, the brush is gently moved back and forth with only light touches making contact with the finish.

A finished dry-brush stroke on the door of a 1990 Chevrolet sport truck. The truck is red, the top pinstripe and dry brush pink and the bottom pinstripe is light green. It is an unusual color combination, maybe, but it is in style and looks great as a finished product.

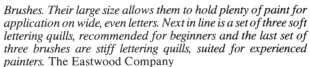

This is a complete set of lettering brushes. The first two on the left are Red Sable script brushes made to produce fine, accurate lines for scroll or signature work. Next to them are three Accent Color Outliners, great for adding second colors and shadows to letters. The three large brushes in the middle are called Jet Stroke

Brushes. Their large size allows them to hold plenty of paint for application on wide, even letters. Next in line is a set of three soft lettering quills, recommended for beginners and the last set of three brushes are stiff lettering quills, suited for experienced painters. The Eastwood Company

Frisket paper has been placed on Dunn's 1935 Chevy panel truck. It has a self-adhesive backside just like self-stick shelf paper. A design will be drawn on it, cut out and used as a stencil. This material can be found at almost any artist supply store.

pany offers full sets of Lettering Quills, Jet Strokes, Accent Outliners and Red Sable Script brushes. Expect a complete set of eleven different styles and sizes of brushes to cost around $70.

Without a doubt, it takes a lot of practice to learn how to effectively paint letters of different script. For cursive letters, just about every stroke is made in an upward motion. Always use a brush that is suitably sized for the job. Brushes must never be too big; in fact, it is better to use smaller brushes and apply two strokes to a letter than attempt to make a large brush fit between lines. For bare block letters, use a brush which is perfect for the width desired. This way, each stroke will complete one part of a letter and prevent the need to make more than one pass.

For the novice, there are ways to paint letters without having to rely on freehand talent. One of the easiest is by way of stencils. You can cut out your own from magazines or from sheets of paper on which you have penciled in certain letters. Professional stencils are available at artist supply stores. Tape these in place securely and simply paint over the cut-out letters. Follow that application with an outline in a contrasting color to make them look even better.

For intricate jobs, professional sign painters use Frisket paper. This material has an adhesive on the back which allows it to stay in place, like self-stick shelf paper. Artists use rulers and other tools to definitively draw their design on the paper while seated at a desk or work table. The drawing is then taken to the vehicle, the

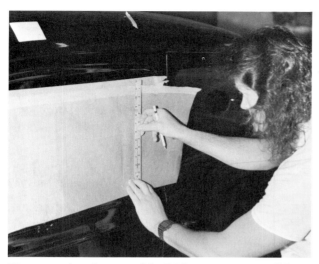

The paper placed on top of the Frisket paper is a stencil Dunn made of his name. Holes have been poked through the name outline with a pounce wheel. A pounce pad will force a fine powder through the holes to make an outline on the Frisket paper. Here, Dunn uses a tape measure to make sure the logo is placed squarely inside the featured truck recess.

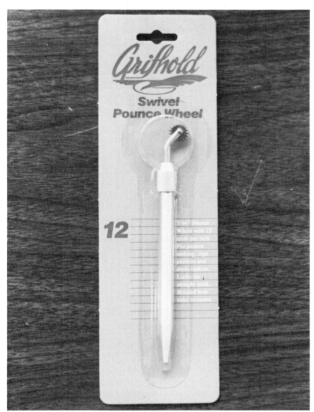

This is a common pounce wheel found at almost any sign or artist supply store. Once a design has been drawn on a piece of heavy paper, its outline will be followed with a pounce wheel. Sharp spikes on the wheel poke holes along the outline through which powder will be forced through, resulting in an outline on an underlying piece of Frisket paper.

Pictured is an assortment of pounce powders and pads. The center cap located in the middle of the pad on the right side is removed and powder poured inside. As the front part of the pad, shown on the left, is tapped along the outline of a pounced design, powder goes through the pounced holes to imprint the outline on whatever is under the design. Powders are available in different colors.

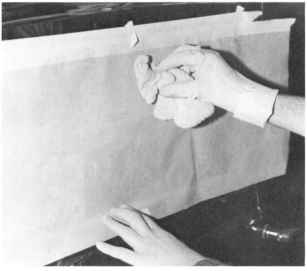

Dunn uses an old sock as a pounce pad to transfer his logo to the Frisket paper. The powder is fine and easily fits through to the other side of the pattern. A great deal of tapping pressure is not needed, just enough to cause powder to come out of the pad. In this instance, Dunn is wearing a rubber glove while using the pounce pad.

It is important to use a sharp blade on the X-acto knife while cutting Frisket paper; dull blades tend to tear the material. Using a metal straightedge, Dunn gently cuts out the pattern left behind after using the pounce pad. Minor cuts may be made in paint but will be covered up with paint for the logo.

As the letters are cut out, Frisket paper is peeled away to reveal the design. Careful cutting is needed around curved corners, and Dunn uses a steady hand. The dark lines located at both the top and bottom of the letters were drawn in with a pencil to guarantee that all letters would be exactly the same height.

backing peeled off and the paper attached where the design is to be painted. Gently using a sharp X-acto knife, painters cut out the design. Then the design section is carefully pulled away from the car leaving behind an exact outline of the custom pattern to which paint can be applied.

Another way painters outline letters or designs on cars is with a pounce pad. Again, with the artist working from a desk or work table, a pattern is designed on paper using rulers and other drafting tools as necessary. Once a perfect design has been created, a tool called a pounce wheel is rolled over the entire pattern edge. A small wheel attached to the handle has spikes located all around its circumference.

As the wheel is rolled across the outline, tiny holes are punched into the paper. After the paper has been taped in place on a car, a pounce pad is taped along all of the holes around the outline. A pounce pad is a porous bag filled with powdered chalk; Dunn uses an old sock for this job. When the paper is pulled off, a light outline is left behind from the powder in the pounce pad. Using lines left by the pounce pad, painters apply paint to create their letters or design.

Actual painting is done with lettering enamel using specific brushes for outlining and filling in. Mix-

The letters have been cut out while the remaining Frisket paper stays to establish a perfect masked surface. This process can be done with almost any design.

ing and matching techniques for the paint and the care of the brushes is the same as for pinstripe operations. If you want to cover your creation with clear paint, for protection and also for producing a higher gloss, be sure to use a compatible clear paint.

Overview

Adding special accents to custom paint jobs can make the difference between a great custom effort and a fabulous one. We have all seen custom cars of similar make and model where one just looks good whereas the other is strikingly more appealing. What was the difference? Could it have been the paint color, scheme, design or was it the addition of subtle accents like pinstripes or outlines around graphics?

Creativity and imagination are the keys. You can do whatever you want to do with tape and paint. The means by which you apply paint and the techniques you employ to lay tape will determine the outcome of any custom paint project you envision.

Be kind to yourself. Don't expect to go out the first time and create the wildest, most appealing custom paint job ever designed. Give yourself time to explore all that has been done before by visiting car shows and reading car magazines. Talk to autobody paint and supply jobbers and custom painters. Visit with local car club members to see who has done what to which vehicle. Have fun. Take your time and enjoy making your car look special, crisp and custom.

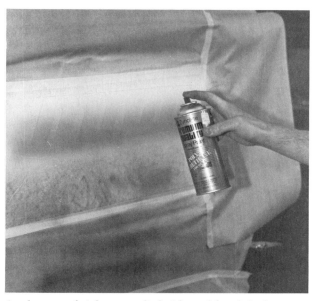

A color coat of pink was applied with an airbrush. It also was a quick-drying enamel. Only the bottom half of the letters was covered entirely with pink, while the top half was lightly coated to allow the top to remain white. Here, a compatible polyurethane clear is painted over the top of the pink and white letters to give them gloss and also for protection.

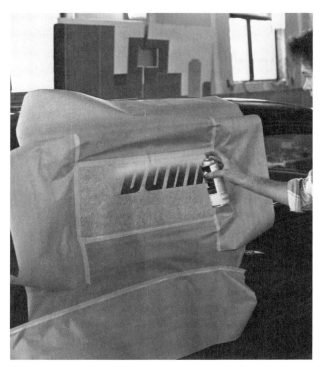

Three coats of fast-drying enamel are applied to the letters. Extra masking is used to prevent overspray onto the vehicle's surface. It is important to use a fast-drying paint for the base to reduce the possibility of runs. Paint runs at this point would surely blemish the entire project.

To help speed paint curing, Dunn uses a blow dryer on medium heat. Too much heat will cause paint to thin out and run; all he wants to do is help solvents evaporate.

121

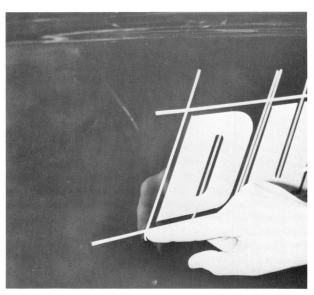

Each letter is outlined with Fine Line tape so that the letter outlines will be perfect. A fingernail is used here to make sure tape is securely attached at the point where it intersects with another section of tape. The line of tape down the middle of each letter also serves as a masking guide for outline efforts.

Frisket paper is gently pulled away from the painted letters. Dunn holds an X-acto knife in his hand to cut out spots where paint and paper are attached. Great caution is used to prevent pulling off flakes of paint and to reduce the chance of paper being dragged over fresh paint.

The tiny blemish on the edge of the inner space is a result of loose Frisket paper. After cutting the design and pulling off required sections of paper, be sure to go over the surface again to make certain all parts of the paper are firmly attached. In this case, Dunn will paint over this edge so the blemish will not be seen.

Excess paint is removed and the brush formed by draping it over the paper cup brim. This brush will be used to form perfect outline borders around all the letters. This is a slow-drying enamel lettering paint that is compatible with the polyurethane clear that already has been sprayed over the letters.

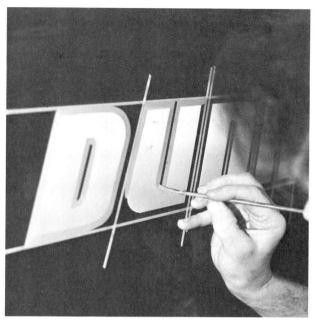

Tape placement was made perfectly and the outline looks great. Freehand efforts were needed around the curved parts of the first letter. After the main lines were painted inside the second letter, tape was pulled so that the bottom section could be completed.

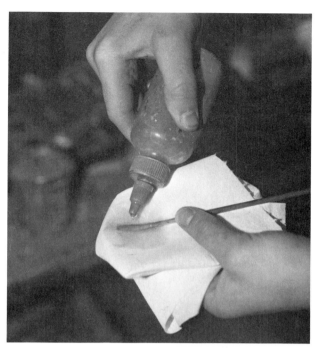

Paintbrushes are cleaned with mineral spirits and a clean paper towel. First, soak brushes with mineral spirits. Then squeeze them between paper towel folds to remove excess paint. Dab again with mineral spirits and squeeze. Continue to work with brushes until all paint has been removed. Squeeze excess mineral spirits out of clean brushes and then dip them into clean motor oil to preserve them.

Tape is pulled off at a sharp angle away from letters. This helps to cut paint as it is pulled. The design looks good, balanced and symmetrical. The rectangular spot on the roof is a business card Dunn is using for reference. More work is needed in order to make the logo complete.

Using a white China Marker, Dunn draws in a hand holding a pinstripe brush. Work has already included tracing a paint can lid and then taping it for the circle and masking efforts for a few lines across the bottom of the logo. Once again, notice the business card located just above his hand which is used as a reference. The logo on the vehicle will match that on the business card.

10

Pinstriping

Almost every custom paint job is complemented, in some way or another, by the talented efforts of a pin-stripe artist. Accents range from one or two subtle pinstripes along a particular body line to colorful arrangements of heartbeats, dry-brush or cartoon-type character images. Most professional pinstripers are genuine artists with a flair for color coordination, an eye for matching designs and a gift for composing images of all kinds.

Experienced pinstripers can complete a series of one or two thin stripes around a car in about an hour or two. This includes setting up, cleaning the car surface, guide tape maneuvers and painting. Other jobs, like extensive lettering and airbrush murals, may require a few days to outline, paint and accent.

As with any profession, there are certain tricks of the trade that help projects proceed quicker and smoother with more defined results and crisper lines. At

Pinstripes do an excellent job of accenting the scallops on this gorgeous High Boy. Almost every custom-painted car is highlighted in some way or another by pinstripes. Colors can be *vividly contrasting or a subtle shade off from the main car color. Widths can also be regulated to conform with the custom-paint design.* Dan Mycon

the base of these tricks is equipment. Along with slow-drying enamel paint, pinstripers use special brushes for specific tasks.

Pinstripe paintbrushes are designed just for pinstripe applications and are not of much use for painting letters. Conversely, attempts to lay down a long, smooth, symmetrical pinstripe with a lettering quill would be fruitless. You have to use the right tool for the job.

As with masking and painting, you must practice pinstriping on a test panel before attempting designs on your car. Watching a professional perform these functions makes the job look as easy to apply as signing your name. Don't be fooled. It has taken professionals a long time to perfect their craft and you cannot expect to equal their talents by just reading a book or watching it done once or twice.

Give yourself some time to practice before putting paint on your car. Get a feel for the equipment and try a number of different creations before settling in on just one certain custom feature. You may decide that a small dry-brush heartbeat will look great on your car or truck, as opposed to a standard unbroken pinstripe around the whole vehicle. You may even choose to

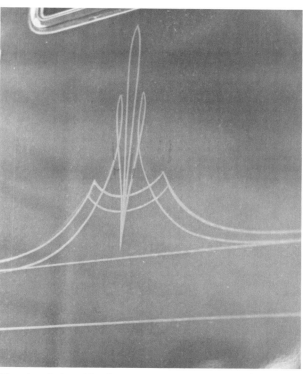

Pinstripe designs like this were popular a few years back. The trend now has shifted toward subtle pinstripes or bold lines erupting into splashes. It is important to consider the era of automobile the stripes are being applied to. Where a pattern like this may look out of place on a sport truck, it may look great on a 1950s Chevrolet.

Pinstripe artists are generally quite talented in more areas than just pinstriping. Dunn freehanded this cartoon character on the tailgate of a custom-painted sport truck. More and more, auto enthusiasts of this decade are including cartoon characters in various forms on their vehicles.

Dunn fills in spears with a contrasting color, as opposed to leaving them open. Although this is a design improvised from an earlier era, it will look great on this spoiler when it is attached to the rear end of its 1990 Geo. Note the unique style of the brush he is using: it is called a sword or dagger and is designed specifically for painting pinstripes.

125

This is Dunn's mobile workbench. All of the tools and materials he needs for any pinstriping or lettering job are kept on the portable table. In lieu of rags, he uses soft paper towels to erase mistakes and clean brushes. Paint is poured into small paper cups for ease of mixing and maneuverability.

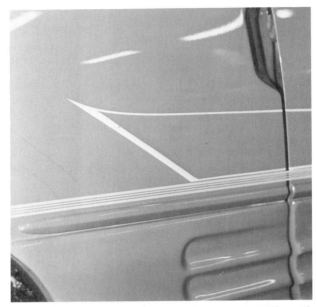

Extra-wide pinstripes require more than one pass. The wide vertical line here was outlined with Fine Line tape and then painted. Tape ensured both sides of the line would be straight. Both horizontal lines were applied using tape as a finger guide only.

The line just above Dunn's hand is Fine Line tape. It is used as a guide that he follows with his extended little finger. The brush is firmly locked between his fingers as his entire arm moves as a unit. The width of pinstripes can be slightly altered by pushing a brush closer to the surface. If only the tip of a brush makes contact, pinstripes will be thin. As more of the bristles' length is laid down, lines become bolder.

The top part of this truck is green and the bottom silver. A wide yellow pinstripe separates the main colors and accents of yellow and black were applied with an airbrush for highlighting.

126

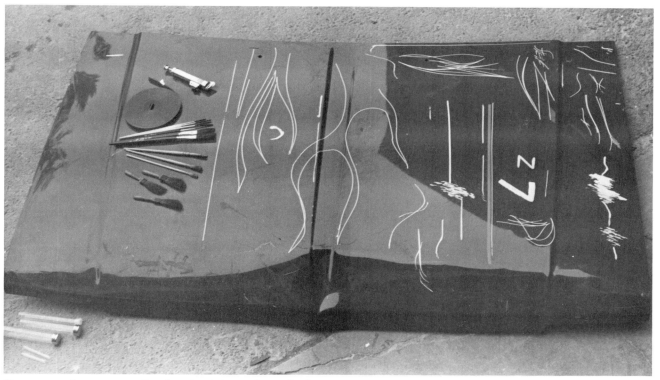

From top to bottom are a Beugler pinstriping tool, a roll of magnetic guide tape, artist's lettering brushes and three dry pinstripe brushes. As you can tell, the novice pinstripers who painted on this test panel need a lot of practice. Practice also includes adjusting paint and solvent mixtures in order to arrive at workable solutions. Tools courtesy of The Eastwood Company

Steve Brown tries his hand at pinstriping while using a length of Fine Line tape as a guide. Notice that the bristles on his brush bend down. This could mean that the paint mixture is too heavy for the brush or that he simply has too much paint on the brush. Bristles should stick straight out for optimum painting results.

In this photo, Brown tries his hand at lettering, a task that appears to be a lot easier than it really is. Again, paint and solvent consistency needs to be adjusted so that the brush flows easily and smoothly. Add a few drops of mineral spirits to a couple of ounces of paint. Practice with it to see how it flows and adjust accordingly with more paint or more mineral spirits.

127

More than a couple of practice sessions were needed before Dunn could consistently write his name like this. He lays down a line of tape at the top and bottom of letters to ensure those edges are straight. Again, the correct brush size plays a significant role and the consistency of the paint used can mean the difference between a clean crisp line and a jagged one.

include some airbrush work for highlighting curves around large graphics. You won't know what you can do until you practice. So break out the old hood or trunk lid test panel and have some fun.

Pinstripe tools
Brushes

In order to put on a long thin stripe in one pass, brushes have to hold a lot of paint. Ordinary artist-type paintbrushes have short hairs or bristles which cannot hold nearly enough material to paint a line more than a few inches long. Pinstripe brushes, called swords or daggers, feature extra-long hairs measuring about 2 inches in length. This allows a user to load the brush with enough paint to make lines as long as 6 feet in one stroke.

These special brushes are found at autobody paint and supply stores, outlets for artist supplies, sign supply stores and mail order businesses, like Eastwood. A favorite brand of pinstripe brushes is made by Mack, available in six different sizes, ranging from #00 to #4.

Although pinstripe widths can be slightly regulated by how far down the bristles are pushed against

Brown is using an artist's brush to apply a dry-brush heartbeat design. Dunn has had better luck using small inexpensive parts brushes for this effort. This design may have turned out better if less paint was put on the bristles and the brush was held at a more acute angle with the surface.

This dry-brush effect was applied using three separate strokes with a small parts brush. Painted on the side of a 1990 Geo, the upswing pattern conforms with the rear body style. Other dry-brush strokes may have worked just as well to fill in the open spot between pinstripes, and this is where individual taste and imagination come into play.

a surface, it is best to use a brush size best suited for the width desired. Pinstripe brush width is designated by numbers, with the smallest number, #00, being the most narrow. As the number increases, the brush gets wider—size #00 is designed for very fine lines, #2 for medium lines and #4 for bold lines.

Cheap pinstripe brushes may save you a dollar or two upon their purchase, but the hassle of working with inferior bristles and ferrules is not worth the meager savings. Pinstripe brush hairs must remain intact as a unit if lines are to be straight, crisp and even. Just one hair jutting out will cause paint to land outside a stripe and look sloppy and unprofessional.

Another feature to consider on pinstripe brushes is the handle. Many times you will want to round off a pinstripe into a curved pattern. This is best accomplished by twisting the brush between your fingers while effecting the rounded line. Square handles make this maneuver difficult. Be sure the pinstripe brushes you buy have round handles, like the Mack brand, to make this effort easier to achieve.

Mechanical tools

For rapid and accurate pinstripe projects, a number of custom auto wholesale companies rely upon pinstripe tools to effect stripes quickly with clean results. One such tool is made by Beugler. Available from The Eastwood Company, this tool features a set of seven different heads which have various-sized wheels attached.

A cylindrical body holds paint and a plunger mechanism forces out excess air. Paint is supplied to a free-spinning wheel which lifts paint from the body and applies it to the surface being striped. Heads sizes range in width from $\frac{1}{64}$ to $\frac{1}{8}$ inch.

The Beugler body features a clasp into which one of an assortment of small guide bars is attached. Used in

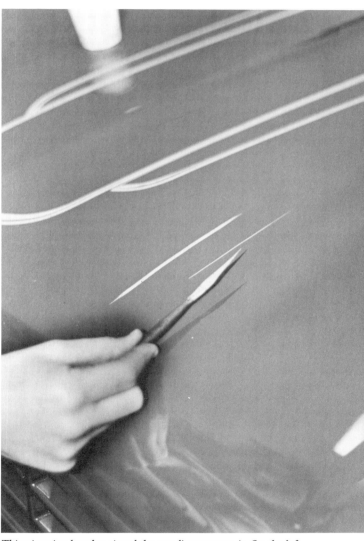

Each line you see was made with one separate stroke of a pinstripe brush. In order for brushes to hold enough paint for long lines, their bristles have to be long. Ordinary lettering brushes do not hold nearly enough paint to make lines as long as the center ones in this design. Steve Brown

This pinstripe brush painted the two lines next to it. On the left, almost the entire bristle length was laid down on the hood surface. To the right, only the tip was allowed to make contact with the hood. Notice how stiff and straight the bristles are. This is achieved through mixing just the right consistency of paint and solvent (mineral spirits).

129

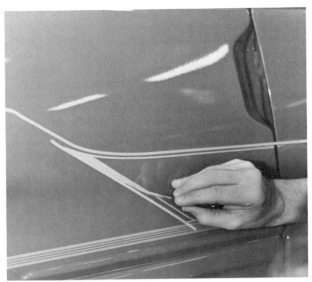

Fine Line tape is used to outline a wide pinstripe. Two passes were required for the pinstripe brush to fill in the entire space. A larger pinstripe brush could have been used, but in this case it was quicker to just apply a second line of tape. The top line is also Fine Line tape that was used as a guide to apply the single top pinstripe. At the bottom, Finesse Pinstripe Stencil Tape is in place, ready for three pinstripes to be painted simultaneously.

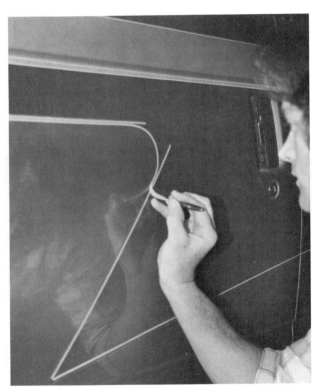

Dunn used the Fine Line tape as a guide while painting straight lines. The arc is made by hand. As he pulled the brush from top to bottom, the brush was twisted clockwise between his fingers. This kind of freehand work requires practice. Until you have mastered the art, you should rely on tape to serve as a guide.

conjunction with a flexible magnetic strip, guide bars follow along the strip to make straight lines. Each guide bar is shaped differently so you can use various ones for following different guides other than a magnetic strip. With a little practice, you will be able to accurately pinstripe along body lines, around fender lips and adjacent to other car sections using body ridges or seams as guides.

This tool works great for making perfect pinstripes. Included with the Professional Beugler kit is a set of detailed instructions with a number of easy lessons geared to help you learn how to make curves and other pinstripe designs. Eastwood offers the complete Beugler Professional Kit for around $90. Magnetic guide strips are available in 15 foot lengths.

Pinstripe paint

Roy Dunn has been pinstriping cars for about fifteen years. He has had excellent results using Sign Painters' One Shot brand lettering enamel paint for pinstripes and a host of other custom paint and lettering creations. This type of slow-drying enamel paint is readily available at sign supply stores, some artists supply houses and through mail order from Eastwood.

This is the Beugler pinstriping tool, complete with seven different heads, five guide bars and a cleaning brush. The 15 foot long roll of magnetic tape is sold separately. Paint is poured into the Beugler body, and air is forced out by way of a push rod. A free-spinning wheel on the head picks up paint and then lays it down on a surface. This tool works great, especially for clumsy novice pinstripers. Tools courtesy of The Eastwood Company

Most professional pinstripers use One Shot or equivalent slow-drying enamels because they go on smooth with superior flow and do not leave telltale brush marks. Lettering enamel's slow-drying feature is perfect for applying long pinstripes, as faster-drying paints would tend to get sticky toward the end of a pass, making application of crisp lines almost impossible.

Dunn uses mineral spirits to thin One Shot paints and to clean brushes. He has also used turpentine successfully. Because most of his jobs only require small amounts of paint to be used at any one time, Dunn has had good luck using small paper cups as paint mixing and carrying containers. For ease of handling, bulk mineral spirits are poured into a small, half-pint plastic jar equipped with a tapered tipped cap. This way, he can regulate the addition of mineral spirits into paint mixtures by drops from the eyedropper spout, rather than having to pour it from a can.

One Shot colors are easily mixed together to create new colors such as red and white to make pink. You can experiment on your own to come up with interesting color combinations. For added help, artist supply stores sell charts which demonstrate how to mix certain colors to arrive at new ones.

Pinstriping techniques

As with any painting endeavor, certain items must be accomplished before actual paint application begins. To start out, you should have the following items readily available: paintbrushes, paint, mineral spirits, ⅛ inch Fine Line tape, paper cups (not plastic), wax and grease remover, rubbing alcohol to diffuse static electricity on plastic pieces, paper towels, and sharp razor blade or X-acto knife.

Start with a clean dry car and then determine which areas will be pinstriped; clean them with wax and grease remover. Dunn, like Laursen, Mycon and Murdock, stresses safety and always wears a heavy rubber glove when cleaning with any solvent, even wax and grease remover. He also wipes off potential pinstripe sections with rubbing alcohol to further clean and dry the surface.

Once the finish of the car is perfectly dry, Dunn lays out a line of ⅛ inch Fine Line tape just above the

With a section of magnetic tape in place, the Beugler guide bar makes it easy to lay down a straight stripe. Adjustment of the bar will allow the tool to make a set of lines equally spaced. With a different head, the second line could be made wider or thinner. Complete instructions and a set of practice patterns are supplied with each kit.

Dunn has had the best results pouring drops of mineral spirits into little paper cups of paint by way of a plastic jug equipped with a tapered spout cap. Since only a couple ounces of paint are used at any one time, just a few drops of mineral spirits is all that is needed for a good mix. As paint thickens, he adds only one drop at a time to thin.

131

To lay down a straight line of tape, Dunn has attached the free end to a spot near the taillight. As the tape was kept taut, he rolled out enough to make his way to the front of the vehicle. At that point, he squats down to get his eye level with the tape line. Carefully, tape is moved closer to the car until it is attached. Attempts are continued until the line is perfectly straight.

site where paint will be applied. He takes time to make sure the tape is aligned perfectly, as if it was going to be a permanent fixture. In this instance, though, tape is simply used as a guide. He has found that tape goes on better if he puts it on rather fast as opposed to going too slow, which will result in jagged lines.

Place tape wherever pinstripes are planned and in any design you wish to create. Just remember that tape should be placed a quarter of an inch or so above the planned pinstripe. It should not be in the way of painting efforts, yet close enough so your little finger will touch it as you run a pass with the brush.

You will not paint up against the tape, rather just below it. If paint were applied against the tape, you would not know how wide the pinstripe would be. By keeping pinstripes in the open, you can easily see how wide the pattern is and adjust as it becomes too thin or too wide.

If you have chosen to use a Beugler pinstriping tool, surface preparation is still the same, except for Fine Line tape application. To set up a magnetic strip—useless on nonmetal car bodies—you will need a yardstick or other soft straightedge. Lay the strip in the general location of where you want to paint pinstripes.

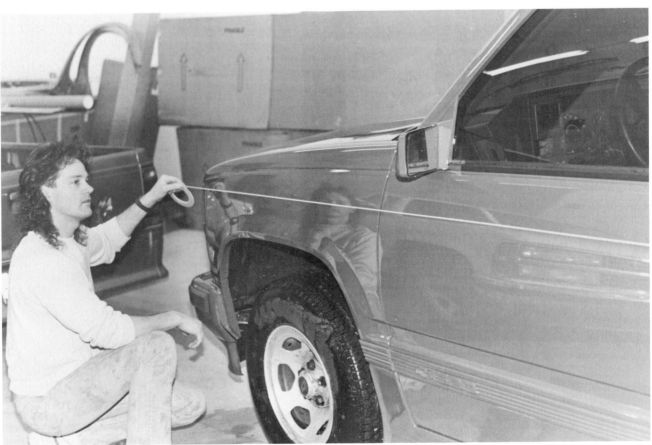

Placing a line of tape for use as a guide is just as critical as placing one for actual masking. As his right hand controls the tape's direction, the left hand secures tape to the surface to secure its position. Dunn says it is better to move a little faster and apply tape in a smooth, free-flowing fashion than to take too much time and get the tape on in jags, bends and dips.

Then use a yardstick to situate the strip in a straight plane. Since the magnetic strip only comes in lengths of 15 feet, you will have to remove it when finished with one side of the vehicle and reposition it on the other side for that pinstriping job. If you plan to use a body ridge, crease or other feature as a guide, you will not need a magnetic strip.

Pinstripe stencil tape

An easy way to apply perfect pinstripes is to use pinstriping stencil tape. Finesse Pinstriping Inc. manufactures Striper Paint Pinstriping Stencil Tape, which, at first glance, looks like ordinary vinyl pinstriping tape.

However, it only comes in one color and is specifically designed as a stencil for pinstriping paint. It comes in twenty-seven different styles which enable custom painters to apply more than one pinstripe at a time in a variety of widths. It is available at autobody paint and supply and auto parts stores.

With stencil tape, individual lengths of tape are covered with a clear film and then combined into a single roll. Individual tape sections come in varied widths and patterns. The entire piece of tape, all separate sections included, is laid on the car with blank spaces denoting where paint will be applied. When the tape has been placed to your satisfaction, the clear film is peeled off to exhibit from two to four separate and evenly spaced pieces of masking tape.

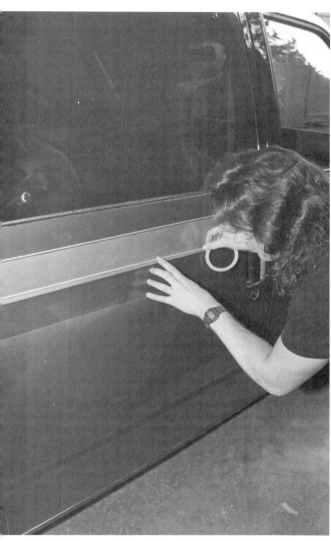

Four different graphics colors will be highlighted with pinstripes. Fine Line tape is in place to guarantee a straight guide edge. The brush will not touch tape, only come next to it. Since pinstripes will now affect each of the colors' paint edge, it is important that the stripe be straight. If the striper were to follow just the paint edge, a small dip or jag would be noticeable. On the other hand, it does not matter how much of the pinstripe covers the painted line edge, as long as there is no gap between it and the pinstripe.

The top line in this photo is Fine Line tape. Used as a guide, it is not critically important that the tape be followed exactly, as shown by the wider gap located at the top of the arc. Straight lines must follow the tape more closely because dips or waves will be easily noticed. Note that the actual pinstripe line is painted just below the guide tape. If paint were to flow on top of tape, its width would vary a great deal once tape was pulled.

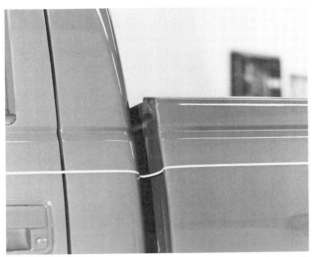

When crossing over seams, like doorjambs or truck bed and cab openings, there is no need to cut tape to fit. Since it is only used as a guide, placement like this shown is perfectly fine. The pinstripe brush will be stopped when the line has been completed up to the gap. Striping is done panel to panel with no stops in between, if possible.

Paint is then applied between them to effect pinstripes. When painting is completed, the tape is removed and the result is perfect pinstripes.

Although Striper tape is available in twenty-seven different styles, you can alter them to create wider lines by simply pulling off one of the pieces after the original full-bodied tape has been applied. Dunn uses this kind of stencil tape when applying multiple pinstripes next to each other (more than two) in order to get lines equally spaced and perfectly matched.

Each stripe can be painted a different color to result in two to three different-shaded pinstripes. All you have to do is carefully paint each line a different color using a thin brush.

Finesse Pinstriping Stencil Tape is an excellent way for novice pinstripers to get started and a great source for all pinstripers applying multiple lines at one time. Twenty-seven different striping patterns are available, some of which can be altered to offer even more of a variety. Dunn uses this product for painting multiple stripes on lower sections of cars where mobility is hampered.

Although this picture seems to indicate four pinstripes already in place, the fact is that no stripes have yet been painted. This is stencil tape in place featuring a design for three equally spaced and identically sized pinstripes. A clear film maintains four separate tape pieces in place. After the unit of tape has been placed, the clear film is lifted off to reveal four separate masking tapelike lines spaced between what will soon be painted pinstripes.

Angles also can be made by intersecting tape sections and then cutting them with a sharp razor blade or X-acto knife. To make a right angle, for example, overlap one section over the other. Then, using a razor blade, gently cut masking tape sections until you have an open line where you want paint applied. Use caution with razor blades; too much pressure applied to them while cutting tape will cut into the base paint. Use only enough pressure to cut the tape, even if such gentle pressure requires you to make more than one pass.

Stencil tape, just like guide tape, is put on straight by attaching the free end to a location desired at one end of the vehicle and then stretching it out to the full length needed. Hold it away from the car's surface a few inches and bend down so that your eye is level with the tape. Then carefully move it toward the car body in the exact location desired, all the while maintaining pressure on the tape to keep it taut and straight. When it has been attached to the surface, stand back to check for its proper alignment. If it is off, pull it away from the car and start over. Continue until the tape is placed exactly where you want it.

Go back over the tape with hand pressure to make sure it has adhered securely. Gaps between it and the body will allow minute drops of paint to enter and ruin an otherwise perfect line. Make absolutely sure no dirt, lint or hair is embedded in the tape because paint will flow under it to cause blemishes. This is really impor-

Using an X-acto knife, Dunn has carefully separated the clear film from the individual tape members. This must be done carefully as to not disturb the placement of any of the underlying tape pieces. Make absolutely certain the tape is placed perfectly before pulling off the clear film. Once the film is removed, it is virtually impossible to adjust the individual tape pieces and also keep them equally symmetrical. Also, be sure no dirt, lint or hair is trapped beneath tape because paint will flow under it to cause a blemish.

When painting over stencil tape, a wide-bristle paintbrush can be used. This is because long, single strokes are not required. You can start and stop as many times as it takes to apply the pinstripes. Go slow, though, so that you do not end up splashing paint over the top or bottom edge of the tape.

tant for stencil tape since paint will be applied a little thicker than with freehand pinstriping.

To ensure super adhesion between stencil tape and a car surface, Dunn always runs his free hand over the clear film just ahead of his other hand which is pulling it off. This extra bit of pressure directly on the tape just an inch or so ahead of the clear film being lifted off guarantees that the masking part of the stencil tape stays in place with no loose air gaps.

Painting pinstripes

Dunn buys One Shot paint in large cans and then inserts an eye screw into the lid. This way, he can pour out just an ounce or two of paint and then quickly seal the can without having to clean residual paint from the groove around the can's top. Paint cans should not be left open as a film will form over the top of the paint and eventually contaminate it with solid flakes.

Color mixing is done in a paper cup. You can experiment on your own or follow instructions from color charts found at artist supply stores or books from the library. For example, blue mixed with yellow will make green, red and yellow make orange and blue combined with red creates violet.

Add a few drops of mineral spirits and stir with an ice cream stick until paint becomes a heavy cream-like consistency. Paint that is too watery will run. Paint that is too thick, like molasses, will not flow evenly enough

As soon as all stencil tape painting has been completed, Dunn pulls off all stencil tape. He figures it is much better to pull it off while the paint is still a little wet than to take a chance with dry paint peeling off flakes of pinstripe. This is a valid concern since the entire area from the top to the bottom of the stencil tape will have been painted, and chances are that it would all dry as a unit.

As he pulls off the clear film from the stencil tape, Dunn uses a finger from his free hand to apply pressure down on the tape to ensure it is attached and to prevent any of the individual sections from lifting off with the clear. This also gives him the chance to force tape down a last time before painting, with a guarantee that every inch has been touched.

to make extra-thin pinstripes. Practicing with a test panel will help you determine a working consistency that flows best for your needs.

Since this kind of slow-drying enamel can easily and quickly be removed from cured auto paint, you can place just a small line on the car to see if the color you have mixed looks right on top of the vehicle's color. Then, simply wipe it off with a soft paper towel dabbed with mineral spirits. If the color is off, make adjustments by adding a drop or two of whatever color will tint it to the shade desired.

Dip the pinstripe brush into the paint and then lap it against the side of the cup to work in a load of paint and shape the bristles. Dunn may work the brush against a side of the cup twenty times before finally lapping it against the cup's brim three to four times for final bristle shaping. Other pinstripers have been known to gently pinch bristles between their thumb and index finger to properly shape them.

Although applying pinstripe paint should not be done in a hurry, going too slow will cause lines to dip, and even the slightest break in a smooth pass will result in a blemished line. You should position yourself in such a way that an entire line can be painted in one motion. This may require you to stretch forward at the beginning and end up stretching in the opposite direction to conclude a pass.

Movement should be made by your arm as a unit, from the shoulder to your fingers. Lock your wrist and elbow in place and make your body move to complete a

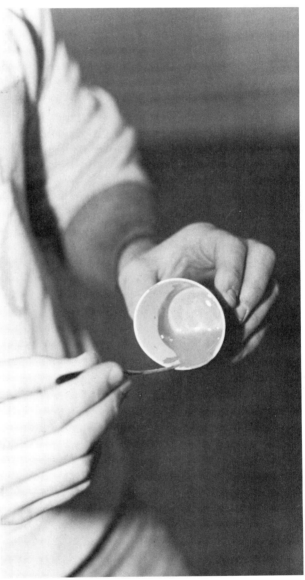

Pouring an ounce or two of paint at a time can really get messy. To prevent the mess, Dunn inserts eye screws into the lids of his paint cans. This way, it is easy to pour out minimal amounts and he does not have to bother replacing lids with paint puddled in the groove along the open edge of the can. This also eliminates the forming of film over the top of paint, a common dilemma when paint is continually exposed to air.

Once a paint and mineral spirit mix has been poured into a paper cup, Dunn laps a pinstripe brush against the cup's side 20 to 40 times. This accomplishes two things: it helps to further mix the paint and also loads up the long pinstripe brush bristles with lots of paint. Satisfied that the brush has plenty of paint, he will stroke it against the cup's brim a number of times to remove excess paint and to form the bristles.

pass. This helps to keep lines straight and reduces the chance that your wrist or elbow might force your hand into an up or down direction.

Your little finger should extend down to touch an edge of the Fine Line tape already laid down just above the pinstripe site. This finger will be your guide throughout the pinstriping exercise, as your hand and arm will be blocking your vision as you proceed. Right-handed pinstripers usually paint from left to right; left-handers from right to left. Dunn always looks ahead before painting so he can see what is coming up.

Paint the line in a definite, controlled motion. Don't hurry, but don't dawdle either. In one second, you should be able to paint a line at least 2 inches long.

If you plan to put a set of two pinstripes one on top of the other, paint the top one first and let it dry before painting the second. This way, you will not accidentally smear the top line while making the bottom one.

Forming spears, points and other pinstripe designs is just a matter of joining the lines together. It does take practice to get lines on opposite sides of each other to match in length and curvature. For a series of accents and curves, start each line at the top and paint down. Attempting to paint in an upward direction is difficult and unreliable. For the most part, pinstripe brushes should always remain in one position in your hand. You can twist them between your thumb and index fingers to make a curve, but do not reposition them to paint upward.

The same holds true while painting horizontally. Always paint back toward the line you just made. For instance, if you are going to apply a set of figure-eights at the front fender to join two pinstripes that run back toward the rear of the vehicle, start from the front of the fender and paint back toward the pinstripe for both sides of the figure-eight. What you will actually paint is a figure like the letter S and then another one shaped like a reversed S.

If a mistake is made, don't worry. Lettering enamel, like One Shot, easily wipes off up to thirty minutes after it has been applied. Pinstripers always carry a soft cloth or paper towel with them to erase mistakes. Yes, even the professionals botch a line once in a while. Should paint begin to dry out and not flow evenly, add one drop of mineral spirits to the paint and stir thoroughly.

Pinstripe care

Pinstripes are not generally covered with a coat of clear paint. There are times when you may want to put a clear finish over pinstripes to smooth out their abrupt edges, like with outlined flames or scallops. Before you apply just any brand of clear paint over lettering enamel, be sure to check with an autobody paint and supply jobber to see which brand is compatible with the kind of slow-drying enamel you used.

One Shot lettering enamel lasts a long time. It withstands weather and resists chalking for years.

Preparing for an extra-long pinstriping stroke, Dunn reaches as far as he can toward the left. He has positioned himself in a way to allow his body to stretch from one end of the bed to the other so that the pinstripe can be made in one unbroken stroke. Notice that the jug of mineral spirits is close by, sitting on top of the far right-hand end of the pickup bed. Also, the paper cup of paint is in his left hand and a clean paper towel in his back pocket.

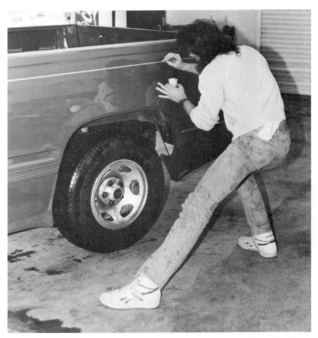

Stretched almost to the maximum, Dunn completes the long pinstripe stroke on this pickup truck bed. Should he have stopped before reaching the end, the stripe could have still been accomplished: he would have simply started the line again an inch or so away from where he stopped. Then, he would have gone back to join the two lines.

However, since it takes so long to fully cure, do not wax over pinstripes for at least a month. After that, refrain from applying polish or other abrasives on top of pinstripes. Too much polishing will break them down and could even erase them after a while.

Since Fine Line tape is used as a guide, there should be no problems pulling it up with reference to pinstripes that were applied near it. However, if you have just put pinstripes on a freshly repainted car the tape could possibly pull off flakes of that new paint. Pull tape just as you would during a graphic design sequence. Go slow and bend the tape back over itself away from the pinstripes.

In the case of pinstripe stencil tape, Dunn recommends pulling it as soon as you have completed that entire striping effort. He feels that pinstripes are less likely to flake while the paint is still relatively wet, as compared to pulling the tape after the paint has hardened. This is because a good amount of paint will have splashed on top of tape to create, in a sense, a layer encompassing the pinstripe and the tape. Again, pull the tape slowly back over itself to create a sharp bend in it to cut paint edges as it is pulled. If a small dab of pinstripe paint has spread beyond its edge, use a paper towel fold dabbed lightly with mineral spirits to wipe it off.

Clean pinstripe brushes with mineral spirits or turpentine. Use a paper towel or soft cloth to absorb paint residue and excess thinner. Make sure every spot of paint is removed, including areas close to ferrules.

When his brushes are clean, Dunn pinches them with a paper towel to remove as much mineral spirits deposit as possible. Then, he dips them into clean motor

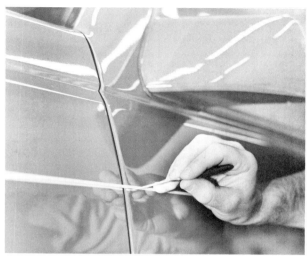

The pinstriper's little finger is resting directly on top of the guide tape, while the rest of the fingers secure the pinstripe brush in place. This is an excellent hand position for applying pinstripes. Note how just the tip of the brush is touching the surface to make a thin line. For added control, the middle finger is resting on top of the brush's ferrule area.

oil, shakes off the excess and lays them flat in a tool chest drawer. Motor oil keeps bristles from drying out and also helps them to retain their distinctive shape. Other pinstripers and sign painters use petroleum jelly in lieu of motor oil.

While painting lines on lower body sections, it is nice to have a section of carpet handy to kneel or sit on. In this position, Dunn's wrist, elbow and shoulder are locked as a unit and his body is forced to move. This ensures an even line without worries about dips, sags or waves.

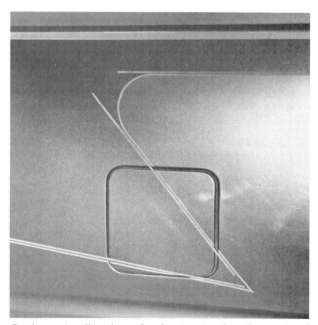

Guide tape is still in place after the pinstripes have been painted. Gaps were left over the gasoline filler door on purpose. Painting over the rubber gasket would have been sloppy and made the lines look crooked. The point was simply made by joining the lines together. Any paint extending past the point was carefully wiped off with a soft paper towel.

Mineral spirits are dabbed onto a spot on the paper towel to remove a little section of pinstripe in preparation for dry-brush work. Slow-drying enamel will easily wipe off in up to 30 minutes—sometimes an hour—after its application. This feature is another reason why it is a perfect paint for pinstripe application.

Pulling the guide tape from a pinstripe job presents no real problems. You should always pull tape away from fresh paint and be careful that sagging tape is not dragged across new pinstripe lines. If tape has been laid on top of a freshly painted vehicle, you might make sure to pull it off at a sharp angle in order to ensure that it does not pull off any paint flakes.

Not satisfied with how the line started out, Dunn simply erases it and will try again. All pinstripers erase lines once in a while. Not every line is going to go on perfectly for you either. Have plenty of patience and keep trying until you paint lines that meet your approval. Rubbing alcohol wiped across the taillight lens will reduce static electricity which can reek havoc with brush bristles as they are pulled across the plastic.

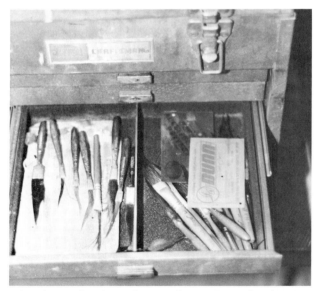

After cleaning brushes with mineral spirits, Dunn dips them into fresh motor oil and then lays them flat in a tool chest drawer. Oil keeps the bristles from drying out and also helps them to retain their unique shape. Other pinstripers have had good luck using petroleum jelly as opposed to motor oil.

11

Troubleshooting and Finishing Touches

Custom paint projects are not totally complete after a color design has been sprayed. Clear coats have to be applied, and sanding is generally needed after that. Lacquer jobs require sanding to remove orange peel and also bring out their rich gloss. Those paint finishes which include a hardener can also be sanded for maximum gloss or orange peel flattening. Straight enamels with no hardeners cannot be color sanded as their finish will be ruined. After sanding, surfaces are buffed or polished to bring out an even higher gloss and to remove lingering sanding scratches.

Troubleshooting

Custom auto painting is not an exact science, as quite a number of problems can arise during a spray session. Stop painting as soon as any imperfection is noticed. You could have an improper paint mixture, the gun could be clogged or any number of associated conditions could be presenting themselves. You have to correct problems before continuing. Otherwise, the entire job may be ruined.

Bleeding

Bleeding is a condition where the surface is discolored, generally caused when new paint is not compatible with existing old paint on the surface. Solvent in the new paint loosens up binders and color in the old paint to let it bleed through.

To solve this problem, you will have to remove all the damaged paint, prepare it for paint again and then spray on a sealer which will protect the old paint from the new.

Blistering

Blistering refers to paint that suffered a multitude of small bumps, like blisters, over the surface. This can be caused by painting over rusty or dirty surfaces, applying second and third coats before solvents in preceding coats have evaporated or by moisture in air lines used to supply the spray paint gun. These areas have to be sanded smooth and then prepared with primer before repainting.

Too much emphasis cannot be placed on properly preparing car bodies for paint. They have to be perfectly clean before paint is sprayed. Additionally, water in air lines will cause all kinds of problems, from blisters to fisheyes. If your air compressor does not have enough capacity to supply required volumes, rent a larger unit from a rental yard.

Blushing

Blushing occurs when moisture is introduced to the surface which is being painted. This is caused by mois-

Mycon's 1988 Chevrolet sport truck sports a European monochromatic custom burgundy paint design. This style calls for all exterior attributes to be painted the same color as the main body, including mirror housings, door handles, grille and bumpers. For further customizing, he has tinted the windows and dropped the body as low as practicality will allow.

141

ture in air lines, moisture on the car body or by painting a car when its surface is cold and the paint is warm. Blushing looks like white splotches mixed in with the color coat.

High humidity can also cause this problem, as moisture becomes prevalent on the car's surface while it is painted over. The situation can be remedied by installing a water trap in the air compressor line, making sure that the car and paint are both at room temperature, or by using a slower solvent.

Cracks

Cracks in new paint are a result of paint drying much too fast or of not waiting the prescribed time between additional paint coats. Rapid drying times are caused by fast solvents and unusually hot temperatures. When second and successive coats of paint are applied too soon, solvents in underlying coats have not evaporated sufficiently and are, in essence, coming out of the new surface by way of cracks.

Other conditions can also cause cracks, which some custom painters may refer to as checking or crazing; these include painting over a surface that already suffers this problem and using incompatible paint or additive mixtures. Always be certain a surface is properly prepared before painting and remember to use a paint system that is compatible, not only with an existing surface, but also with all of the materials you use together for new paint.

Fisheyes

Fisheyes look like small circles where rings of paint have formed around a central point. The major cause of this problem is silicone contamination. If you can, clean that section of paint before continuing. Be sure to use a quality wax and grease remover and consider a second or third cleaning with an ammonia-based glass cleaner. If that does not work, you will have to add a fisheye eliminating product to your paint mix. Once that mix has been made, use it throughout the entire painting project.

Lifting

Lifting paint looks similar to paint that has been covered with a paint stripper—all wrinkled. This can be caused by applying a new paint over one which is not compatible, like lacquer over an enamel that had not been mixed with a hardener. This problem requires that bad paint be removed and the entire repaint system done over again.

Problems like this can be avoided by talking with your autobody paint and supply jobber right from the beginning. If you plan to paint a new custom design over existing paint, you have got to be sure that the new paint is compatible with the old. If you don't, you may discover that all your efforts have been wasted and the whole process has to be done over again. This time, though, you will also have to spend a considerable amount of time stripping off all of the damaged paint.

Mottling

Mottling is a term that describes a color problem. In essence, a mottled paint job is one that looks streaked, like different colors were put on in varying shades. This condition is caused by inconsistent paint application; some passes were put on heavy, others too thin. To solve this problem, if noticed in time, you can apply another coat in a more uniform fashion. On those surfaces that have dried, sand as needed and apply new paint.

Orange peel

Orange peel is a common paint problem which describes a finish which looks like the bumpy texture of an orange peel. This happens when paint is applied too dry. The cause can be related to an improper solvent (too fast) or holding the paint gun too far from the surface.

For lacquer and paint with hardeners, this imperfection is sanded out with a fine grit paper. Uncured enamels must be rubbed out with either rubbing or polishing compound.

If orange peel starts to show while you are spraying, check to see if you are holding the paint gun more than 12 inches from the surface of the car body. What is happening, in this case, is paint actually starts to dry before it reaches the surface. Thinner or reducer can also cause paint to dry too fast. If you are using a fast

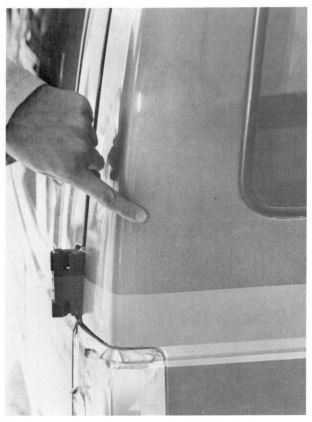

Mycon is pointing to a paint edge left behind after custom graphics were applied to his wife's van. Ordinarily, clear paint would have been sprayed over the line and feathered into the unpainted pillar section. In this case, though, he plans to add black from the line to the roof edge in order to match black around windows and on other pillars.

solvent on a hot day, chances are that it is evaporating too fast, resulting in orange peel.

Runs and sags

Runs are caused by holding a paint gun too close to the car body, by painting on a dirty surface or by using solvents that are too slow for ambient temperatures. Runs and sags occur when too much paint is applied to the surface and all of the binders are unable to attach themselves properly.

Fix this problem by readjusting your gun position, cleaning the surface more thoroughly and by using a solvent designed for the temperature range which currently exists in the painting area. If you discover runs early on, wipe them off with rags and an appropriate solvent. Make corrections as needed and try again.

Wet sanding

In some cases, custom painters may carefully wet sand multicolor paint edges to remove build-up before clear coats are applied. This can only be done on solid colors with no additives mixed in. Sanding colors which include candy coats, metallic flakes or pearl will ruin the even disbursement of layered tints or special addi-

tives. Sanding efforts for these are done on their clear coats only.

To develop super glossy, rich finishes, painters sometimes wait up to three weeks for clear coats to cure before their final sanding efforts. Directions listing the number of clear coat applications for each paint system (sometimes up to eighteen) and their curing times before sanding are clearly displayed on information sheets and product application guides. These sheets also commonly include recommendations on which sandpaper grit to use with each wet sanding endeavor. Most often, though, sanding starts out with 600 grit, with final sanding done with 1200. Use straight strokes only, and never sand in a circular motion or across a surface; that is, always sand from the front of the car toward the rear, not side to side.

In order to help sandpaper cut quicker and resist clogging, lightly spray surfaces with a diluted mixture of liquid dish soap and water before sanding.

Before you start ripping off masking paper and tape, be certain all required clear coats have been ap-

While wet sanding the roof of Dunn's 1935 Chevrolet, Mycon sprays on a mixture of water and mild dish soap. This helps wet-and-dry sandpaper to cut quicker, last longer and resist clogging. Note that he is using a wooden paint stir stick as a sanding block while sanding the rounded edge of the roof.

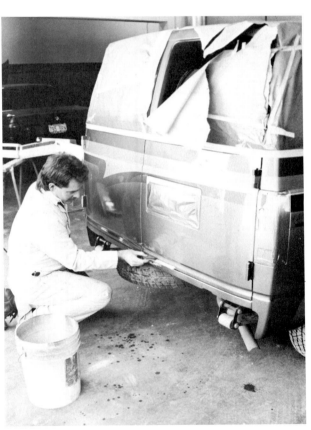

Although the painting operation appears to be completed on the van, Mycon has left masking paper and tape in place while wet sanding and polishing efforts are underway. Paint blemishes might be found that require extensive sanding and will have to be repainted with clear. In this photo, Mycon is again using a paint stir stick to wet sand parts of a body groove located at the bottom of the rear doors. Note the bucket of water for wetting the sandpaper.

Using a buffer, Mycon polishes areas that were wet sanded and others that need a little buffing out. A soft pad is attached to the buffer and 3M Imperial Microfinishing Compound Liquid is the polish in use. Special care must be given to buffer operations, as just a slight slip of the machine is all it takes to burn through paint clear down to primer.

A large variety of rubbing and polishing compounds is available at autobody paint and supply stores. On the left, is 3M Super Duty Rubbing Compound used for compounding auto finishes to a high gloss. On the right, is DuPont's 101S Lacquer Rubbing Compound, a product designed for hand application only. The degree of coarse grit contained in a compound designates its polishing strength: products designed for hand application have much more grit than products for use with buffers.

plied. Although Mycon and Laursen are always excited to see a custom project stripped of masking, they generally wait until all sanding has been completed. This way, masked parts are protected against scratches from an accidental slip with a sanding block and are covered in case more clear is needed after sanding.

Buffing and compounding

After a paint finish has been wet sanded, you will need to rub it out with compound to remove sanding scratches and further bring out the deep rich shine so familiar with custom colors. A number of various compound products are available at autobody paint and supply stores.

The most abrasive polishing agents are called compounds, such as polishing compounds and rubbing compounds. Their use is intended for initial buffing efforts to remove harsh sanding scratches and minor orange peel remnants. As the job continues, less abrasive products are used which will further polish out minor imperfections to leave a brilliant shine.

Custom painters commonly start with an abrasive compound for heavy work and then graduate to a finer

Mycon has spread a line of compound on the fender flare and is ready to operate the buffer over it. Buffing along ridges and corners must be done carefully in order to prevent buffing completely through the paint, creating a paint burn. Many custom painters quickly turn the buffer on and off by pulsating the trigger to keep the pad speed slow while polishing these items.

polish for finish work. Your autobody paint and supply jobber can help you with the proper selection of compounds, some of which may be individually recommended for specific paint systems.

Laursen has had good results using 1200 to 1500 grit sandpaper to remove dirt and flaws from clear coats. He follows that with an application of Meguiar's #2 and then Meguiar's #9. His paint finishes are swirl free and look great.

Power buffers save lots of time and energy while polishing paint finishes; they are used commonly in professional autobody paint shops. Polishing compound is applied to the paint surface through a squirt bottle or wiped on with a cloth. The buffing pad is then operated over the top of the compound in areas about 2 feet square.

Since buffing maneuvers can quickly and easily remove paint from ridges, corners and edges, operators have to keep the machine under control at all times. Novices should use buffing machines with a maximum of 1450 rpms; anything with a faster pad speed should be saved for experienced professionals.

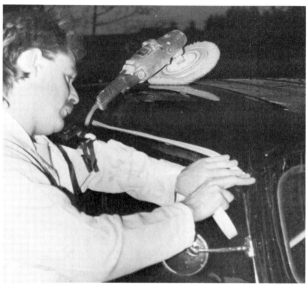

Extensive buffing was required along the edge of Dunn's Chevrolet. To be certain he doesn't buff through the paint, Mycon is placing a piece of masking tape along the drip-rail edge. This is an excellent idea for all novices who lack experience with buffers; novices should protect all ridges and corners with masking tape.

Buffing the lower sections on cars and trucks poses an awkward working position. Here, Mycon has chosen to sit down while performing the function on his van. Notice that he has switched hand positions in order to work in this position. The same procedure could be accomplished standing up by simply reversing the position of your left hand on the handle extension, with your thumb pointing out instead of next to the machine.

The best assortment of quality buffing pads can be found at autobody paint and supply stores. A few different styles are available depending upon the type of buffer you use. Pads come in various textures, some designed for heavy-duty polishing and others for lighter work. To arrive at a good combination of buffing pads and compounds, check with your local auto paint jobber.

Laursen has had good luck using a Schlegel #1 pad with Meguiar's #1 Professional Machine Cleaner. This combination works well to flatten orange peel and bring out a high gloss.

Schlegel's #2 pad and Meguiar's #3 Professional Machine Glaze combine a less coarse pad and polish for removing minor paint problems and producing an extra-high gloss.

Using an abrasive compound with a power buffer will make quick work of polishing clear coats. To reduce the chances of paint burns (removing paint down to primer), many custom painters place masking tape over ridges, around corners and along edges. This protects paint on these vulnerable areas from a rapidly spinning buffing pad. These areas are polished later by hand.

An assortment of buffing pads is available at autobody paint and supply stores. Cutting pads are designed for heavy polishing to remove stubborn sanding scratches and orange peel. Finishing pads are used with less-abrasive compounds and can even be used with creamy waxes for final buffing. After a buff job with wax and a finishing pad, painted surfaces should be smooth as glass, glossy and sleek, like a sheet of ice.

Masking tape removal

In your zeal to see the overall results of the custom paint design you have just put on your car, do not get carried away by wildly pulling off masking tape and paper. This is especially important when pulling tape after an initial coat and re-applying it for another segment.

Paint edges may be high along the tape edges, and pulling the tape off in a haphazard way could ruin an otherwise perfect edge. A tiny chip could be pulled off, or an entire flake.

Pull tape backwards and away from the paint. This will create a sharp bend in the tape which helps to cut off high edges. Go slow! If you notice paint sticking to

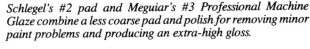

Using the clean end of a paper matchstick, Mycon applies leftover original paint to a chip on a Chevrolet Crew Cab. Paint is just lightly dabbed into place to effect the repair. You can also use an artist's paintbrush to accomplish the same task. Be sure to repair nicks as soon as you find them; deep chips could expose bare metal to oxidation and rust problems. Once rust gets a hold on metal, it travels under paint and will eventually cause extensive paint blistering, flaking and peeling.

146

both the surface and the tape, use a new razor blade or sharp X-acto knife to gently separate paint and tape. If your design includes sharp points like flame tips, start tape removal from the widest spot first and gradually work your way to the tip.

More often than not, especially on multilayer color schemes, paint edges come out rougher than expected. This is not to say that large flakes will peel off when you take your time and pull tape back on itself and away from the painted part, but the edges may be just a little jagged. The problem is easily solved with the stroke of a pinstripe brush.

Most colorful designs look better when they are outlined with a contrasting color, or even with a shade that varies slightly from the pattern itself. Look closely at other custom paint jobs and notice how well a carefully applied pinstripe accents the overall scheme.

Overview

The variety of custom paint designs available to car owners is limited only by the imaginations of those who apply them. Car enthusiasts have used acetylene torches to create smoked effects on paint and have spent literally weeks applying coat after coat of various colors to produce a finish comprised of dozens of colors in dozens of patterns.

Nothing is impossible as long as you work within the guidelines set by paint manufacturers. The chemists have developed paint systems that will adhere as

The bow-tie was painted pink and the 1500 emblem is being painted a light green to match the pinstripes Dunn applied to this 1990 Chevrolet sport truck. Notice that the size of the paint-brush he is using is just a little smaller than the width of the numbers. For this kind of finish work, it is better to go over a surface twice than to have to maneuver with a brush that is too big.

expected and last a long time when properly applied and maintained. It is up to you to follow the instructions set forth by information sheets and product application guides.

Professional custom painters may have their own ways of doing things, which may not always fall within the recommendations of manufacturers. However, their experience has enabled them to learn how certain items work with others and how projects can go faster using different techniques. Novice custom painters lack experience and therefore should follow established guidelines.

Dunn is dressing up the red monochromatic paint scheme on this 1990 Chevrolet sport truck by painting the bow-tie pink. This little trick has been done by a lot of Chevrolet owners to break up a solid color just a little. Dunn is using an artist's paintbrush and One Shot Lettering Enamel on this job.

A pink pinstripe has been continued over this taillight lens. Many auto enthusiasts have included this kind of pattern over headlights as well. The only caution here is to not get carried away to the point where paint decreases the candlepower of the lights to make them illegal.

12

Paint Care and Detailing

When you have completed a custom paint project, your vehicle's interior, trunk, engine compartment, fender-wells, wheels, tires and underbody may be covered with sanding dust, or may generally appear dull and lacklus-ter in comparison to the freshly painted body. Slight amounts of overspray may have inadvertently gotten on tires, fenderwells and underbody assemblies, or these parts just may appear neglected. In order to bring these items and the rest of the car up to the same impressive standards of its newly painted body, you must detail it.

Auto detailing is a systematic and conscientious cleaning and shining of every part of a vehicle's interior, exterior, engine compartment, trunk and underbody. Professional painters frequently hire experienced de-tailers to clean customers' cars after extensive body-work and paintwork. Detailing makes the overall repair job look its best. You can spend a few hours or a weekend detailing your automobile to perfection; how far you take it is up to you.

The wrinkled texture on this paint denotes orange peel. Depending upon how deep it is, block wet sanding and additional coats of clear will remove it. Final compound buffing will leave the surface glossy and orange-peel-free. This type of orange peel is common with lacquer paint jobs, but wet sanding will flatten the surface.

Art Sukut's classic 1966 Chevy II L–79 is in concours-winning condition. Driven only on fair-weather days, every square inch of the vehicle is pristine. Although this car does not feature wild graphics, flames or scallops, its paint finish is custom because it was applied with meticulous care—and kept that way.

148

Concours d'elegance winners spend hundreds of hours cleaning every square inch of their competition cars, including the tops of transmission cases and bell housings. They are the elite breed of all auto detailers, driven solely by a passion for perfection and a special enthusiasm for flawlessly prepared and maintained automobiles.

Custom paint jobs should last a number of years, especially if quality products were used throughout the process. But their lasting beauty and glossy finish will not endure prolonged exposures to harsh weather and penetrating sun rays unless properly maintained and protected.

Waxing new paint

An adequate coat of quality carnauba-based car wax is probably one of the least expensive and easiest-to-apply methods of protecting automobile paint finishes against ultraviolet sun rays, water spots and airborne pollutants. Along with a frequent (weekly) washing schedule, you should plan to wax your car or truck at least once every three months or any time water fails to bead up on the paint surface.

Murdock believes that wax helps to protect all paint finishes, even the bulletproof urethanes. Besides, road oil and other debris always seem to come off of a freshly waxed surface much easier than off other, non-waxed finishes.

Paint manufacturers often specify certain waiting periods that designate how long their paint system should cure before wax is applied. This time frame allows solvents to thoroughly evaporate before the surface is sealed with wax. Information sheets, product application guides and autobody paint and supply jobbers should be able to furnish you with this information. Normally, sixty to ninety days is recommended.

Although the instructions on many car wax products suggest application be made in circular motions, Mycon and Laursen, among other auto enthusiasts, have found better results applying wax in straight, back-and-forth movements. This straight pattern greatly helps to reduce swirls and allows better control while working next to emblems and trim. Wax along pinstripes and paint edges as opposed to over them. This will reduce the amount of wax build-up between the actual paint edge and the body.

Apply wax with a soft clean cloth or square sponge slightly dampened with clear water. Small rectangular household sponges work well. They are a manageable size and their straight edges allow you to bring wax up to seams, badges, trim and lights without smearing over them.

Wipe off dry wax with a soft clean cloth. Cotton towels, old flannel shirt remnants and cloth baby diapers work great. Long-time auto enthusiast Art Wentworth buys pure white flannel by the yard at fabric stores. Those sheets are cut into smaller sections for wax removal. When they become soiled, he simply puts them into the washing machine and dryer. They come out clean and even softer than they were when new.

Remove dry wax using the same straight back-and-forth pattern as you did when applying it. To get wax residue out from light trim and emblems, use a small paintbrush with the bristles cut to about ½ to ¾ inch. Short stout bristles work fast to dislodge dry wax and their soft texture will not scratch paint.

As far as poly-glycoat and other no-wax paint preservatives products are concerned, Mycon, Murdock, Dunn and Laursen shy away from them because their silicone or silicone-like ingredients make touch-up and repaint efforts a tremendous hassle.

Washing new paint

Lacquer paint and those which included hardeners should suffer no ill effects from early washing. To be sure, check with the jobber who sold you the paint system you applied. However, washing a new paint job in direct sunlight, especially if paint is physically warm or hot, may surely result in water spot blemishes. Never wash cars in direct sunlight and always allow the car's body to cool down before spraying water on it. In extreme cases, cold water applied to exceptionally hot car body surfaces will subject paint to thermo-shock, a condition which will actually cause paint to crack.

Use soft cloths, towels or mitts for washing. Mycon uses wash mitts made from cotton. They are found at auto parts stores and are labeled under the name Chenille. Synthetic wash mitts may cause minute scratches or swirls on paint finishes. These swirls are obvious when the vehicle is parked in direct sunlight.

Extended use of synthetic materials will eventually cause spider webbing, a condition characterized by thousands of swirl lines which look like dozens of spiders walked across the car's surface and left behind a layer of webs. To get sanding dust or dirt out from tight spaces around grille work, light fixtures and trim, use a soft bristled floppy paintbrush.

The type of soap used for washing cars, especially those with new paint, is important. Soap products designed just for car washing should be fine since they were developed for car bodies and auto paint finishes. Mild liquid dish soaps also work well. Granulated soaps present somewhat of a scratch hazard if each granule is not completely dissolved.

Dry new paint surfaces using soft, clean towels. Cotton fabrics work best for drying and also for reducing the chances of swirls. Save chamois materials for other jobs. They tend to collect dirt and grease and pose potential scratch or blemish hazards.

Polishing new paint

If a new custom paint job is conscientiously maintained, the need for abrasive polishing should never arise. There are times, maybe once a year, when you will want to clean the paint surface thoroughly and remove any old wax build-up. In those cases, use a mild polish.

Meguiar's manufactures a wide variety of auto polish products. Each container includes a definitive label which describes the type of finish it is most suited for. For newer painted surfaces with no oxidation problems, there is no need for aggressive polishing.

Therefore, use the mildest polish available and settle for repeated applications of that product to gently remove wax build-up and to shine slightly dulled finishes. Just one application of a harsh abrasive polish will remove minute paint layers unnecessarily and will require additional application of a milder polish to remove swirls.

Pinstripes and other accents that have not been covered in clear paint should be spared from anything other than extra-mild polishing efforts. Lettering enamel resists oxidation quite well but continued polishing maneuvers over such paint will eventually erase it. Use the straight edge of a soft sponge to control polishing passes up to but not over pinstripes, accents and other features applied with slow-drying enamel.

Protection from ultraviolet sun rays

Other than sheer neglect, nothing seems to destroy quality custom paint jobs faster than continued exposure to direct sun rays. Parking in the shade is great, provided it is not under a tree. The use of a quality car cover made with a material that breathes will greatly increase a paint job's longevity.

Meguiar's offers a wide range of auto polish and wax products. Definitive labels describe just what kind of paint surface each product is designed for. The best selection is generally found at autobody paint and supply stores.

If you are forced to park your car in the sun day after day, you should protect it with a car cover. If, for some reason, you cannot use a car cover, then at least alternate parking arrangements so that one side gets the bulk of sun one day and the other side on the next day. You could back in to a parking space on the first day and then pull straight in the next. At least this will prevent one side of the car from baking all the time while the other remains shaded.

Repairing nicks, chips and scratches

Automobiles that are driven on normal roadways will suffer paint chips and nicks. There is nothing you can do to prevent it; unfortunately, they are inevitable.

A good coat of wax may be just enough to prevent minor nicks. Bras will certainly help to protect against chips, but they can flap in the wind to cause scratches and if left in place for long periods will collect all sorts of dirt, grit and debris underneath which will vibrate against paint to cause scratches. If used at all, put a bra on just before driving on an unusually bad stretch of road and then remove it when back to good pavement conditions.

Paint nicks and small chips are touched up with paint left over from the original job. Car enthusiasts have used the clean end of paper matchsticks for years to apply paint to nicks. You can do the same or use a fine artist's paintbrush like those used for lettering and outlining. Dab on just a little and let it dry. Then apply just a bit more if needed. It is better to apply two light touches than one heavy glob.

This is quite easy for small blemishes. When touch-up paint has cured, polishing compound can be used to smooth slightly rough finishes. Follow up with a mild application of fine polish to remove any lingering swirls.

If your custom paint job was done with candy, pearl or a metallic paint system, touch-up work will not be as visually attractive as for solid colors. It is impossible to touch up candy colors as there is no way to accurately match the color or number of paint layers needed to effect its tint and depth. About the only thing you can do is dab on some clear and live with minor nicks and chips. At least the clear will prevent oxidation of underlying sheet metal and help resist rust.

Pearls and metallics should be touched up with the same paint used for its application. Although pearl and metallic additives will not perfectly match what is on the car, the color will be the same. This should be enough to adequately cover imperfections and remain more or less unnoticed.

Large paint chips and scratches will have to be sanded and repainted. Deep scars that expose bare metal will have to be primed, shot with primer-surfacer, sanded and repainted. Medium blemishes that have not damaged anything but the paint can be sanded and repainted with minimum efforts using the same techniques applied while conducting the original custom paint finish.

To repair minor chips and scratches, those not much bigger than a pencil eraser, try this technique. Mask off the area of the chip and lightly sand with 400 to 600 grit sandpaper. Masking tape will prevent sanding on top of surrounding paint. Apply one light coat of touch-up paint. Allow it to set up and then apply another, always staying within the confines of masking tape. Continue to apply paint until the surface of the touch-up paint is slightly higher than the surrounding paint. Then pull off the masking tape and allow the paint to dry for at least a week.

After a week, mask the spot again. Use fine sandpaper to smooth the paint chip repair until it is just about the same level as the surrounding paint. When it has been sanded to nearly the same height, remove the masking tape and apply polishing compound to the chip and surrounding area. Polishing will feather the repair into the surrounding area. Finish off with fine polish to remove swirls. The repair should be unrecognizable.

Detailing

Sanding dust is best removed with a vacuum cleaner. Use a bristled-brush attachment with long hairs to remove dust from cracks and crevices on dashboards and along door panels. Regular heads are used for carpet and upholstery.

Mild cleaners, like Simple Green, are used to remove dirt and grease smudges. To prevent excessive overspray, dampen a cloth with cleaner and then wipe the surfaces. Use caution around new paint; enough time has really not elapsed for full curing and certain cleaners could stain freshly painted finishes.

If masking tape adhesive has stuck to certain spots, use a mild solvent to dissolve and remove it. Clean the spot again with cleaner.

Paint or primer overspray on glass is removed with mild solvent or a razor scraper. Try using solvent first, as scraping with a razor could possibly scratch glass or nick rubber moldings.

Overspray on tires or other rubber surfaces is removed with solvent. Stubborn patches may require the added strength of a scouring pad with solvent. Be sure to wash those rubber pieces with plenty of soap and water to remove any residual solvent. To replenish the gloss and luster on vinyl and rubber parts, Laursen prefers to use Meguiar's #40. He likes this dressing better than others because it does not contain much silicone.

Fenderwells and other underbody areas should be cleaned and then painted as needed. Dirty fenderwells are a real eyesore. Nothing detracts from a super custom paint job, crisp tires and interesting wheels than fenderwells the color of dry dirt. If nothing else, clean them with a heavy water spray and plastic scrub brush. Allow to dry and then spray them with black paint. This will help the entire vehicle look crisp and stand tall.

Under the hood, the plastic sheet you placed over the engine should have prevented sanding dust from building up on the intake manifold or any part in the engine compartment. If some did sneak in, use a damp

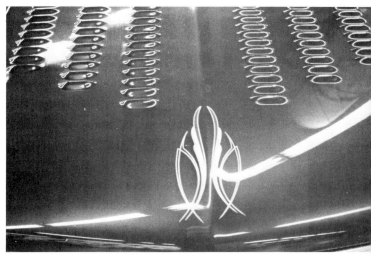

Aggressive polishing over pinstripes can eventually erase them. Slow-drying enamel, the paint used for most pinstripes, will last a long time but not against harsh polishing with coarse abrasives. Unless there is a definite need to polish pinstripes, save them for wax coverage, not polish.

cloth to wipe clean. A slow water flow from a garden hose, along with brisk agitation from a floppy paintbrush, should work quickly to remove dust and dirt. Stubborn dirt or grease spots are removed with Simple Green or a similar cleaner. Do not splash or flow water on carburetors, distributors or computers. Moisture condensation in these units can cause engines to run rough or could prevent them from starting at all.

Paint chips and nicks are easily touched up with the clean end of a paper matchstick. After your custom paint job, be sure to keep leftover paint handy. Use it to lightly repair chips and nicks to keep the finish looking good and to protect underlying sheet metal from the elements of oxidation and rust.

Index

Acrylic enamel paints, 21–22
Acrylic lacquer paints, 22–23
Adhesion promoters, 36–37
Air compressors, 49–51, 109
Airbrush cleaning, 111
Airbrush techniques, 109–110
Airbrushes, 109–112

Bleeding, 141
Blistering, 141
Blushing, 141–142
Body parts removal, 60–62
Buffing, 144–146

Candy paints, 25–27, 92
Clear coats, 23,
Clothing, 56–57
Cobwebbing, 112–113
Color blending, 105–106
Color choice, 48–49
Compounding, 144–146
Cost estimates, 39–40
Cracks, 142
Custom painters, 39–41

Designs, 7–18, 71–72
Detailing, 151
Determining old paint types, 59–60
Dry-brush techniques, 115–117

Enamel paints, 21–22

Fiberglass preparation, 69
Fisheye eliminators, 34
Fisheyes, 142
Flames, 73, 105
Flash times, 106–108
Flexible additives, 34
Fluorescent paints, 28
Frisket paper, 118–123

Glass cleaners, 68–69
Gloves, 53–56
Goggles, 56

Hardeners, 25,
Heat guns, 62–65
High-volume, low-pressure (HVLP)
    systems, 31, 51–53, 96

Imron DuPont urethane, 24
Isocynates, 22, 24

Lace painting, 112
Lacquer paints, 22–23
Lettering, 117–123
Lifting, 142

Masking a design, 72–80
Masking equipment, 47–48
Masking paper, 48
Masking tape removal, 123, 146–147
Masking tape, 47–48
Masking techniques, 70–83
Metallic paints, 27, 107
Monochromatic styling, 113–115
Mottling, 142

Nitrocellulose paints, 22

Orange peel finishes, 142–143, 148
Overspray protection, 81–83

Paint and solvent mixing, 87–90
Paint application, 84–108
Paint booths, homemade, 44–45
Paint care, 148–151
Paint coats, 92–94, 108
Paint curing, 85, 121
Paint gun cleaning, 96–105
Paint gun maintenance, 96–105
Paint gun techniques, 90–105
Paint guns, 51, 84
Paint repair considerations, 17–18
Paint strippers, 37–38, 62–65
Paint suppliers, 41–43
Paint thickness, 108
Paint types and properties, 19–31
Paint-gun-to-surface distance, 94–96
Painting tools, 44–57
Pearl concentrates, 27–28
Pinstripe stencil tape, 133–136
Pinstriping brushes, 128–129
Pinstriping care, 138–140
Pinstriping mechanical tools, 127,
    129–130
Pinstriping paint, 130–131
Pinstriping techniques, 131–133
Pinstriping, 124–140
Polishing new paint, 149–150
Pounce wheel, 119
Powder coating, 115
Power sanders, 46–47

Preparation, 58–69
Primer-surfacers, 35–36
Primers, 34–35
Priming techniques, 67–68

Reducers, 20–21, 32–34
Repairing chips, 150–151
Repairing nicks, 150
Repairing scratches, 150–151
Respirators, 53
Retarders, 32–34
Runs, 90, 143

Safety considerations, 25
Safety equipment, 53–57
Sags, 143
Sandblasters, 66
Sanding blocks, 46
Sanding equipment, 45–47
Sanding techniques, 65–67
Sandpaper, 45–46
Sealers, 36–37
Silicone problems, 69
Solvents, 20–21, 87–90
Splash designs, 74,
Spray patterns, 91–92, 95
Spray sequences, 93
Stencils, 80, 117–123
Support chemicals, 32–38

Tape-paint designs, 79–80
Test panels, 85, 86–87
Thinners, 20–21, 32–34
Troubleshooting, 141–147

Ultraviolet ray protection, 150
Undercoats, 34–37, 67–68
Urethane paints, 23–25

Vehicle use considerations, 8–9
Ventilation, 45
Volatile organic compounds (VOC),
    20, 29–31

Washing new paint, 149
Water traps, 49–51
Wax and grease removal, 68–69
Wax and grease removers, 37
Waxing new paint, 149
Wet sanding, 143–144
Work area, 44–45
Wrinkle finishes, 113